It's Not
Business
It's
Personal

ALSO BY RONNA LICHTENBERG

Work Would Be Great If It Weren't for the People:
Making Office Politics Work for You

THE **9** RELATIONSHIP PRINCIPLES
THAT POWER YOUR CAREER

It's Not
Business

It's
Personal

Ronna Lichtenberg

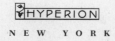

NEW YORK

Library of Congress Cataloging-in-Publication Data
Lichtenberg, Ronna.
    It's not business, it's personal : the 9 relationship principles that power your career / by Ronna Lichtenberg.
        p. cm.
    ISBN 0-7868-6594-6
    1. Interpersonal relations.   2. Interpersonal communication.
3. Success in business.   I. Title.
    HM1106. L53 2001
    650.1'3—dc21

Original hardcover design by Jessica Shatan   00-061311

FIRST PAPERBACK EDITION

Paperback ISBN 0-7868-8513-0

10 9 8 7 6 5 4 3 2 1

For my mom, Bess Glaser,
the best teacher I ever had about relationships;
and my dad, the late "Judy" Glaser,
whose voice still lovingly demands performance.

CONTENTS

It's Not
Business
It's
Personal

INTRODUCTION

I BET YOU'VE HEARD THE PHRASE "BUSINESS IS BUSINESS," OR "IT WASN'T personal," or "you shouldn't take it personally." You hear phrases like this all the time, which is why you may be surprised to find that you've just opened a book that argues for an entirely different perspective.

Not only do I believe that much of business is personal, but I promise you that if you accept this premise and commit to managing your worklife with this in mind, you'll have a much better chance of addressing the burning need you have in your worklife right this minute.

- You're working 24/7 for a start-up and *your burning need* is for the company's valuations to hold up just a little longer.

- You're working for yourself, at home, and still scared about how you are going to make this plan of yours work. *Your burning need* is to somehow get clients and to get them to send you checks.

- You hate your job. *Your burning need* is to figure out how to make a living doing something else, once you decide what you would like that to be.

- You're done with school. *Your burning need* is to find a job that isn't one you'll regret for the rest of your life.

- *Your burning need* is to drive the company's revenue line up, because unless that happens, they won't pay you enough to cover the kid's braces, let alone another car.

- *Your burning need* is to figure out the answer to the question that wakes you up at 3 A.M.: "Why, if I am so smart, aren't I more successful?"

- *Your burning need* is to figure out how to do your job well and still have a life that includes more time for family and friends.

If you see yourself in the above, this book can help you. It will teach you the nine principles you need to practice every day to build trust-based business relationships. People are what lie at the heart of your needs. That's why building better relationships can get your burning needs fulfilled—money, success, time.

If you practice the nine principles, you will enjoy work more, you will get your work done faster, your days will be less draining, you will find more opportunities, you will have people you can really turn to for support when you need it, and you will get the true feedback you need to be successful in business.

WHY SHOULD YOU BELIEVE THIS PROMISE?

There are a lot of gurus running around and even more management consultants. On top of that there are highly competent psychologists and psychiatrists, sociologists, anthropologists, lawyers, media mavens, business school professors, and big names from every arena who talk about related subjects. You should listen to them, try out their advice, and believe it if it works.

You should listen to me in the same way. Here's why these principles are worth a try:

1. The principles are based on discussions with people you've dreamed of talking to.

I spent almost two years talking with the best in every business about their business relationships—from the banking community to restaurants to spa owners to dot-com marquis. Where else can you hear from Edgar Bronfman, Esther Dyson, Hollywood producers and directors Richard Donner and Lauren Shuler Donner, high-profile CEOs like Bill Pollard of ServiceMaster and Bernie Marcus of Home Depot, and phenomenal entrepreneurs like Nancy Evans and Barbara Corcoran?

Take a look at the cast of characters at the end of this book. These are the people who most inspired me.

I talked with people who were unquestionably successful. The interviews were with practitioners who are masters at relationship issues.

I wanted to go beyond business category ghettos. Since the topic goes beyond CEOs, or large companies, or women, or start-ups, or entrepreneurs, or either coast, I wanted to do the same. My goal was to be as wide-ranging as possible, to sample, to see if what I was learning in one interview held true in another.

What I eventually discovered was that the process itself—selecting interviewees, getting them to agree to the interview, talking with them, following up—was a hologram of the relationship-building process I was trying to find. That learning, too, is reflected in the following pages. I can safely say that through these individuals, I've learned from the best, and, with this book, you can, too.

2. My experience is front line, profit-and-loss oriented and current.

My career has ranged from operating the equipment that seals the ends of plastic dry-cleaning bags together to running the strategic planning and marketing functions of corporate giants.

Whatever hat you're wearing now, I've probably worn it, too: I've been a temp, an employee, a free agent, a middle manager in a large bureaucracy, a senior line executive and a CEO. I've hired, managed, and fired others; launched new businesses; met payroll; and helped others do the same.

Not only do I know that business is about making a profit, but I'm involved in helping my clients and myself run more profitable businesses virtually every day of my life.

As I mined the interviews for insights that led to the principles, it was from this practical perspective: What am I learning that other people can use?

3. I know a lot about what doesn't work.

Lord knows I'm not holding myself out as an expert in relationships in the sense that I always get it right. In fact, it is because I have seen business relationships—including my own—handled so badly that I developed a passion for learning how to do it better.

Those of you who read my first book, *Work Would Be Great If It Weren't for the People*, know that I had a complete education about how complicated business relationships can be.

Once the book was published, though, the floodgates opened. As a result, I hear from people around the world, around the clock, about what a tough time they are having with other people when all they want to do is make a living. Their questions have taught me a great deal. Most important, it became clear to me that those people who focused solely on the defensive posture necessary for dealing with office politics were missing something big. Business relationships are about much more than office politics, they are about cultivating something very powerful.

So What is a Business Relationship, Anyway?

A. An interaction at work that other people gossip about

B. An oxymoron

C. The only possible explanation for why that creep who plays golf with the boss is more successful than you are

D. An ongoing set of interactions between two people with the potential to influence at least one of their livelihoods

E. All of the above

The cynical answer is E, but cynicism isn't helpful here. So we are going to focus on D, because it offers the most opportunity.

Let's start with a couple of definitions. Any initial business interaction is actually a transaction.

A transaction happens when two people complete an exchange of goods and/or services for money.

When one of those two people expects or hopes there will be future transactions and that those transactions have significance for his or her livelihood, that's the beginning of a business relationship. A relationship goes beyond transaction because of the time horizon—it always includes some thought about the future. And it differs from transactions because the interaction isn't complete—someone is thinking, maybe in a small way, in the back of his mind, that maybe the other person could be interesting or helpful some day.

In some business relationships, you influence someone else's livelihood: when you are a consumer, for example, or a passive investor. That's an interesting topic, but this book only speaks to it indirectly.

The focus of this book is about the most important kind of business relationship, the one you have with people who buy what you have to offer and influence your future livelihood.

Let's take the definitions of transaction and relationship for a test drive, just to see how they play out in the real world.

I'm in my red Ferrari convertible (hey, it's my fantasy, I can do what I want). I see your lemonade stand. You offer to sell me a glass of lemonade. The sun has made me thirsty. I take the lemonade, give you money, drink it, drive away, and never see you again. That's a transaction.

Now let's go on to a business relationship.

It turns out that I start stopping at your lemonade stand every day around lunchtime. You remember my name; I learn yours. One day you offer me a cookie from your lunch because I'm grumpy about being hungry. The next week you sell me a sandwich. Around Labor Day, I start thinking that as the weather gets cooler you will need something else to do, and you'd be a great person to add to my team.

We've never been in each other's homes. We don't know each other's family or friends. But we each have expectations of the other and the potential to have a real impact on the other's success. We are at the beginning of a business relationship.

I first learned about the power of relationships when I was in grade school. My family owned and operated a bar and restaurant in the small town of St. Joseph, Missouri, called the D & G—a neighborhood place that attracted an incongruent mix of customers: Families with children frequented the simple-fare restaurant in the back, and serious drinkers congregated in the tavern in front.

The D & G was a blue-collar bar in the 1960s, and my dad was a Jew. It was not always a comfortable combination. Dad needed to keep a blackjack behind the bar for when customers got out of hand.

There was one customer whom everyone called Toughie. Mean little bastard. I don't to this day know if he really had a name. It was just Toughie. He looked a little bit like Ernest Borgnine, and when he had too much to drink, which was often, he got bitter, then rowdy, then downright mean. And I mean *mean*.

One night, after several hours of throwing back Irish whiskey with beer chasers at a bowling team meeting, Toughie's vicious side came out, and he picked a fight with my dad by making some sort of anti-Semitic slur. Dad came at him, and Toughie threw a punch. Dad slipped and fell to the ground, hitting the back of his head, hard. Toughie was on top of Dad in a second, pummeling him with both fists. People who were there said that they were sure Toughie was going to kill him. If he didn't, it wouldn't be for lack of trying.

Then another customer, Gil—who was one of the regulars and a part-time bartender, one of Dad's favorites, and one of the sweetest men I have ever met—stood up. Gil and my father went back a long way.

Gil was himself a big man: He was a telephone linesman, so he was big, strong, and wiry from climbing all those poles. He was one of the few people who had the guts, let alone the physical strength, to take on Toughie.

Gil said: "If you pick up your foot to stomp him, you'll have to deal with me." By this time, not satisfied with pummeling my dad, who was completely out of it from hitting his head, Toughie was obviously considering upping the ante to kicking, or what we called "stomping" in those days. Like most working men, Toughie wore big iron-toed boots. Toughie considered Gil's statement and raised his foot anyway. Gil stepped forward.

Toughie said, "This is none of your affair."

Gil replied, "I'm making it my affair."

Toughie thought it over. He backed off.

Ultimately, it led to this: Gil's sister died in an automobile accident, leaving two children whom Gil and his wife, Zell, adopted. One of them is a charming, well-spoken and hardworking young man named Pete—and Dad went on to take Pete into the business as a bartender and teach him the ropes.

And when it was time for Dad to retire, he sold Pete the business. So now, if you come visit the D & G in St. Joseph, Missouri, you'll see behind the bar not only Pete, who still owns and runs the business, but pictures of my dad, of Gil, and of Mom, holding out plates of food to a group at the annual picnic. There's even a picture of Toughie.

Pete says that, when faced with a difficult business decision, he still thinks of my dad and asks, "What would old Julius have done?" My dad is gone, but the business lives because of business relationships that worked forty years ago.

The investment that Gil and Dad made in each other still creates value.

· · ·

A business relationship differs from a personal relationship in that what we do for a living—or what we might do—provides the connection. This doesn't mean that business relationships can't morph into personal relationships, or that the reverse can't or doesn't happen all the time. But in friendships, what the other person does for a living is not the *basis* of the connection. The connection is shared experiences and passions: fanaticism about a team, or porcelain King Charles spaniels, or kids in the same grade at school, or admitting to a clandestine fondness for Howard Stern. There will be more, much more on friendships in Principle Two! So for now, let's just leave it with the point that business relationships are those connections that revolve around how you make money.

More Today than Yesterday

Is there room in our new millennium, e.com world for relationships? Some folks would tell you there isn't, that all that matters is performance and speed. There are even people who will tell you that being polite in an e-mail takes too long and is therefore unbusinesslike and unprofitable. And it is quite true that building relationships not only takes place over time, but takes time.

So let's look at the speed issue. Americans are on the move. According to a recent article in *The New York Times* by *Economist* writer Adrian Wooldridge, the average thirty-two-year-old employee has already worked for nine different companies in his or her career. In 1999, an astonishing seventeen million Americans quit their jobs to pursue other ventures. That's eleven *million* more than the number who quit their jobs a mere six years before.

It's no surprise, then, that as I write this, one of the hottest management issues around is retention. Thirty percent turnover rates are the norm in e-commerce. Law firms, management consultancies, and businesses of all stripes are trying to figure out how to get people to stay.

For the twentysomethings coming into the workplace, this is business as usual. It seems somehow quaint that their parents ever believed that devoting their lives to a one-track, one-employer ca-reer was the way to go. The workplace rules have changed.

As technologies have freed us to work whenever and wherever we choose, the terms of employment have followed suit. The old-time pension plan, which was explicit about the reward for sticking it out, has been replaced by the 401K, which makes it possible to roll on and still collect your just reward later. Offices? How about a laptop, a Palm Pilot, a cell phone, and a physical space to call your own if you happen to be in the neighborhood.

This constant motion contributes to the attitude that we're all in this alone. We can't trust a company; we can't tie ourselves down. We need to be flexible, portable, fungible, and able to re-define ourselves at the drop of a byte.

As my contribution to speed, on the next page is a quick sum-mary of the changes in the unspoken rules of the career game over the past twenty years.

The only problem is that all this speed has made us, to use a high-tech word, *kludgy*, which is how computer folks describe mis-matched systems. As we whiz by one another, we don't really connect. Which means that every decision is more complicated, takes longer, and is less intelligent because you can't get real in-formation about business problems from people you don't trust. Or, as the immortal saying goes, "The faster I go, the behinder I get."

What's also fascinating about much of this activity is that it is designed to reach an old-fashioned goal: more productive relation-ships with customers, because relationships are often what justifies the difference between generic and premium-label pricing.

A few years ago, my husband and I took a hiking trip in the South of France. We planned and piloted the trip with the help of a guidebook that I started to refer to as "the book of tortures." It was a British book, and very charmingly written, but perhaps not as helpful to American novices as I would have liked, with instructions like "Turn left at the cairn." Until that trip, I thought the cairn was something that belonged in the loo. So, what under

OLD RULES	NEW RULES
Don't make waves.	Make change.
Play your part on the team.	Who's on the team today?
Kick the competition's butt.	Kiss the competition's butt, because they may also be a client.
Don't question your boss.	Make sure your boss knows as much as you do. At least in public.
In the long run, it will all work out if you play by the rules.	What long run?
Your work life and your personal life are separate.	Your work life never stops.
You need to be at an office to communicate.	You need to be awake to communicate.
The boss is in charge.	The boss is in trouble.
The needs of your department are paramount.	What's a department?

normal circumstances should have been a two-hour hike, usually ended up taking us all day. We knew that once we set out, we wouldn't see anyone else until nightfall.

This led to our beginning a ritualistic activity for each day: Right after having a luxurious French breakfast, we would begin preparations for lunch. My husband's job was to carry lunch in his backpack—so our enthusiasm for French food and for planning sumptuous meals in the French wilderness was tempered only by my husband's concern for the muscles of his lower back.

One morning we were in a town called Gourdes, and it just so happened that we were there on market day. We arrived early in the small town square as the market was being set up in order to buy our groceries for lunch.

It was everybody's best stuff. There was the cheese man, the butcher, the lady with the fresh honey, the lavender merchant. There were flowers, and homemade wine, and fresh sausages, and fabrics, and pottery, and freshly baked breads and rolls.

I was just overwhelmed by the beauty of the marketplace.

Yes, it's true, it was France, it was romantic, it had all the smells and energy and flavors of life itself. But it also embodied for me, so clearly, the spirit of free exchange and the open marketplace. It was all there: everybody bringing forth the best that they had to offer; and then the interplay of who they were, and what they had to sell, and who their customers were, and how the other merchants helped or hindered their efforts.

I was truly moved by what an amazing human construction the marketplace is, and what an amazing thing it is to see the relationships in the market coming to the surface and affecting the business.

I watched the interchanges: Would one cheese man, sold out of Camembert, send a customer to one of his competitors? Or would he run over and get the cheese himself? Who was able to go to whom to get change? I watched one butcher who would not talk to any of the other butchers, but would talk to the baker. I watched the negotiations as the stalls were set up: Allied businesses—cheese and bread, meat and wine—tried to set up near one another for their customers' convenience; and certain merchants tried very hard to be near certain other merchants. I watched as customers very deliberately chose the merchants with whom they would deal, based on what seemed to be a complex internal calculation that included the quality of the merchandise, the prices at which they were offered, and the welcoming attitude of the merchant.

We think of the marketplace as impersonal, but in fact it is intensely personal. And the smallest element of the marketplace is the one-to-one relationship. It can't get any more personal than that. Many of us like to fool ourselves into believing that our incredibly complex digital, global marketplace has nothing to do with what goes on in the little square in Gourdes, France. We can be deceived into believing that our world is now too efficient for relationships, that when every bit of information, and virtually any product or service, can be bought with a click of a mouse, the need for relationships has disappeared.

But in fact, it has become even more important.

Think about this: I heard an ad on the radio yesterday that said, "Had a bad day at work? We have four hundred thousand jobs listed on our website . . ." And, yes, while that ad has a humorous tone, it represents a phenomenon that's massively significant. Employees now know what their options are and can easily determine whether or not they are getting what they deserve in every way. Many of these job-search websites don't just give you listings, they give you search criteria, postings, and chat rooms with which you can discuss any one of those four hundred thousand jobs and the quality of life issues surrounding them. In other words, you can find out in advance if your prospective boss is a jerk, what the people are like, and whether or not the place sounds right for you. You can find out with ease what the company's record is in advancing people at your level, whether or not people who have left the company have nice things to say, and, of course, what the company's policies are concerning things that may be of importance to you. And that level of information and qualitative analysis is now available for virtually every service and product for sale in the world.

In the marketplace at Gourdes, if one butcher treats another unethically, their options are limited, and they probably will still continue to do business together or, if not, one can move on and open shop in another town. But in the global marketplace, if you're a jerk, there's no reason for other people to continue to want to do business with you. Their options are endless. Plus, if you do something truly unethical, chances are the details will be posted on websites and circulated to people in your field within moments.

Today we just use different words to describe classic business relationships like the ones I witnessed in Gourdes. We want customers who are sticky, who aren't clicking through too fast. We want a greater share of their wallets and their minds. We want top-of-mind brand positioning. We want intimacy, to keep clients longer by proving that we know their likes and dislikes. We want to own their awareness during the time they spend in their car, or on-line, or in line. In other words, much of what we are all paid to do today is to try to create relationships.

What all of this means is that going fast in and of itself is not the answer. The answer is to go fast only when going fast improves performance, to know when to go fast and when you need to slow down just a little.

As in the old days, results count, and among the most effective tools in business are relationships. In order to win at the game of business, you need to play by your own rules, but never all by yourself. Wherever you are and whatever you're doing, keep in your mind a picture of that little marketplace. Even if you're sitting alone at a computer terminal and feel as if you have as much in common with a cheese man in France as you do with an astronaut on the moon, remember that your business relationships are as personal, as vital, and as crucial as those taking place in a village market—whether it's obvious or not. Which brings us to the nine key principles for every business relationship.

The Nine Principles
This book is organized around nine principles that emerged from my interviews with successful people. The principles are operating guidelines. They are there to help you decide what to do, and with whom, as you go through your business day.

The chapters are ordered in a way that works for me, but you should feel free to start wherever you wish. My order starts with how to think about relationships and moves to what to do with them. If you're really impatient, start midway, because the ideas will feel more concrete and offer more tips.

Here they are:

- Principle One: Always remember it pays to be personal

- Principle Two: Observe the rules of the role

- Principle Three: Be fluent in both pink and blue

- Principle Four: Choose your people like you choose your stocks

- Principle Five: Diversify your holdings

- Principle Six: Don't waste time on the wrong people

- Principle Seven: Do it every day

- Principle Eight: Give yourself time to win

- Principle Nine: Do deals based on relationships

By reading this book, you'll find out more about the principles and how successful people use them. You'll also learn how the principles help you build one of business's most powerful assets: a personal board of directors. Now it's time to learn how to create your own board and boost your career with relationship power.

Always Remember It Pays to Be Personal

"There are very few people who can get through life based on their brilliance and their top performance that can ignore relationships. And if they do, you don't wanna know 'em anyway."

—JEFF MAURER

I HAVE NEWS FOR YOU: HOSTILE TAKEOVERS AND HOSTILE BUSINESS are things of the past.

To thrive today, you need relationships, and they need to be quality relationships. Relationships have always been important to business. It's just that in the last half of the twentieth century, the prevailing business model made them easier to come by than they are today. It was the norm that once you got out of college, you went to work and stayed with the same company for thirty years. No matter how big a company was, after thirty years you got to know people. And you could do pretty well if the only people you knew were the ones with whom you worked. Loyalty counted. It didn't look good to be a "job-hopper." Even if you sort of slowed down after thirty years, you could still get by for a while. As one commercial banker said to me of the predownsizing world, "What's changed is that they used to let us carry our dead."

Today's market is fluid. Not only do people come and go, companies do, too. Mergers, acquisitions, rightsizing, rapid growth, expansion virtually and globally—even if you stay in one place, the people around you don't.

Institutional Relationships Is an Oxymoron

The paradigm has been stood on its head. The organization man was all organization and little man. Now smart companies know the degree to which individuals, and the individual's ability to create relationships, are often the engine that drives their company's value.

Martin Yudkovitz, President of NBC Digital Media and Executive Vice President of NBC, said, "You know, individuals often have enormous authority, more than the company they work for really intends for them to have. They might not have the authority to make policy, but if they're simply the one person who gets along with a client or a partner company and has the ability to gain trust and take a risk and make things happen, it often doesn't matter what the company intends—the person can have enormous influence. NBC acknowledges and encourages pushing authority as far down as possible."

> "Smart companies are the ones who facilitate their employees' key relationships."
> —DORIS MEISTER

Of course, that sort of vulnerability can be terrifying to some companies, as opposed to Martin Yudkovitz's description of NBC, which is why they often intentionally or inadvertently do everything they can to get in the way of relationships. When that happens, they are destroying their value, which can be as costly as the loss of a valued client. Through not encouraging relationships, they are closing the door not only on opportunities for the company, but also on helping their employees grow.

Michael and Ellen Brooks of MB Productions told me a story about how when Michael worked for a large firm selling large-screen video services, he built up a relationship with a particular client, who was based in Nashville. "I went down there, met with them, gave them a long presentation, and built up a relationship with them. At some point thereafter I left the company, and when my client from Nashville called the home office and asked for me, he was told I was unavailable, and they transferred him to someone else. Over and over, all they would say was that I was unavailable; they wouldn't tell the client I had left the company.

"The client tracked me down and offered me his business. I explained to him that I was no longer working for that company—but he said, 'If you want to try to figure out how to do this on your own, you've got the contract.'

"I had built a good relationship with this client, but certainly my former employer, by lying to him and misleading him and trying to usurp the relationship, had made his defection from them to me even easier."

Randy Kirk, President and Co-Owner of Kirk-Murphy Holding, Inc., with ownership of nearly two dozen Taco Bell franchises, knows that relationships are essential to a company at every level. He told me an incredible story of how one woman's relationship skills really made a difference not just to one of his Taco Bell franchises, but to a town.

The story took place during a big hurricane in Daytona. One of Randy Kirk's Taco Bells sits right across the street from the Daytona Speedway. "Hurricanes are like snowstorms: Everybody wants to call in. Nobody wants to show up to work. In fact, hurricane parties lead to enough alcohol consumption that some folks don't turn up for a couple of days. So employers lose a lot of time and money.

"But this time it was different because of the shift manager, Linda Birch. Linda discovered that unlike many of the other stores, Taco Bell still had power after the storm had blown through. And so she got people in there to open: Her staff came in because it was Linda making the call, and they particularly liked her.

"It made the front page in the local paper. The electrical crews, all sorts of emergency relief people, had no place to eat except Taco Bell.

"On top of that, Linda did a seven-thousand-dollar day, which was her best ever. It was a tremendous achievement. She got the award for outstanding achievement for the Daytona market. I'm telling the story at Christmas dinner, everybody in the room is standing up, people are crying, everybody is so supportive of her. It's a great story. But that's the kind of energy and commitment that you get when you treat people right."

After he told me this story, I asked him about the connection between relationship and performance, and he told me, "I think you step from one to the other and back continually. You get the job and you start building a relationship. The relationship enables the performance. The performance then can move the relationship to a higher level. And as you move up, the sophistication between the relationship and your performance continues to mature."

At big or small corporations, intense, personal relationships are what keep clients and customers. As an employee, you must learn how to build these relationships to rise within the company. As a company leader, you must value these relationships because they are your revenue.

Whenever you hear "It's just business, it's not personal," you're hearing an excuse: a justification for someone who is about to do, or has just done, something that doesn't quite sit right. You're hearing that in this instance, profit matters more to the person uttering the phrase than you do. You're hearing the hope that you won't get "emotional," which means angry or hurt. And you're hearing it from someone who's not really at the top of their personal game.

Why do I say that? Because I know that people who are most successful in business, who run huge corporations or have started entrepreneurial enterprises of their own, know that in all ways, if you're looking for long-term success, the truth is: **It's not *just* business, it's personal**. They know that true success comes when you dare to make it personal. By making it personal, I don't mean making it about you. "Personal" means making it about someone else.

Shelly Lazarus, whom *Fortune* magazine named one of America's five most powerful businesswomen in 1999, is the Chairman and CEO of advertising powerhouse Ogilvy & Mather Worldwide. She told me an amazing story about founder David Ogilvy, who died just after the company's fiftieth anniversary.

Shelly went to visit him in his chateau in France just before she was promoted to chairman. He was eighty-five years old and hadn't worked actively in the agency for the previous twenty years. He talked quite a bit about himself and about the old days at the company, as was his style. In fact, Shelly said that he was quite well known for coming across as somewhat less than humble when talking about the business and his role in building it. But that day, quite contrary to character, he criticized himself. Shelly told me that his biggest regret was not spending all of his time going out and recruiting new, incredibly talented people, and making sure that the ones who were in the agency were happy. He felt that he should have spent even more time making sure the people in whom he saw the greatest long-term potential were being challenged, were feeling successful, were getting what they needed, were being nurtured. In fact, he told Shelly, "That's what I should have been doing one hundred percent of the time."

Don't Be Seduced by the Dark Side . . .

Of course, there is another kind of success, but this book won't teach you how to find it. This book is not for cowboys. It's not for people who believe that they can go off by themselves, guns at hips and make money without giving a damn about who gets hurt or who comes along for the ride. It's not for people who believe in the Al Dunlap style of management—Dunlap, of course, is the former head of Sunbeam who wrote a book called *Mean Business* that extolled his philosophy: Cut costs, take no prisoners, screw 'em, and reap all the profits you can. His nickname,

"It's all relationships. And ninety percent of it is the intangibles. Herb Kelleher has said that from day one . . . that the intangibles are ten times more important than tangibles."

—COLLEEN BARRETT

"Chainsaw Al," was earned on his previous job at Scott Paper, where he fired over 10,000 people and 75 percent of the front-office staff. When he was interviewed for USA Today, he posed for a photograph dressed as Rambo in pinstripes, complete with automatic weapons and bandoliers.

Dunlap made a lot of money. Now, however, after being summarily fired by the Sunbeam board for running the company into the ground, he allegedly lives in a high-security mansion in Florida, where, according to Barron's, he has loaded weapons stashed in various rooms and dogs guarding the house, paranoid about all the enemies he's left behind.

People do make a lot of money with Dunlap's methods—at least in the short term. There are people for whom that will be enough. If you admire Al Dunlap and want to have a career like his, good luck to you: now put this book down.

On the other hand, if you want to have a career like the man who replaced Dunlap, Jerry Levin, Chairman, President, and CEO of the Sunbeam corporation, then you need to learn the value of making it personal.

Levin told me that when he took over Sunbeam "it was like a world record loser. The company had lost a billion dollars in 1998. And it was a small company in 1998. Our reputation with the retailers was that Sunbeam was the worst company they had been dealing with. The worst company they had *ever* been dealing with."

During Levin's first week, he called a meeting of everyone in the company and explained who he was and what he was going to try to do. He talked to them about things like his view of accountability, how he thought people should be rewarded, how he would make decisions.

At the same time, he urgently needed new, talented managers to start rebuilding the company. There was no hope of doing it the traditional way with a formal recruiting program. He knew the company's reputation was so troubled that people wouldn't even accept headhunter calls if they heard it was for a position at Sunbeam.

I couldn't imagine the pressure of this level of turnaround, so I was really curious about how he had managed to assemble a team fast enough. Levin said, "In addition to taking advantage of the talent already at Sunbeam, we picked up the phone and we made a lot of phone calls and about ninety percent of the management people we hired were people we worked with before—people who know me, who I knew, who trusted me when I told them that I believed we had a real shot at doing something important here.

"We put together a team who knew me and who knew each other. That was so important to our task, because we didn't have much time, and we just knew what we were doing because we had done it together before. We trusted one another, and we just came in and went to work."

In other words, they came because of the relationships—with him and with one another.

This story is only one of literally thousands I have heard about the powerful career impact of positive business relationships.

Investing in Business Relationships

It's time to begin talking about **investing in relationships for business**—the people we work with, want to work with, and who can help us champion our careers.

Maybe it's a bit cynical to think of relationships as investments—as something to do in order to increase your own level of success. But maybe it's also a bit naïve to pretend that they don't have value in a business context. And it seems to me more than a bit foolish to ignore an aspect of your business life that can prove to be so critical.

One of the most financially successful people I talked with was Morton Meyerson, Chairman and CEO of 2M Companies. Mort, as his friends and

> "Relationships provide you with information. You hear that there's a great new director working, so you check out his movie; you find out who the new writers are; you hear about a new script, and someone you trust tells you it's great, so you read it, and you buy it. It's all about the information, and you find out everything through people and relationships."
> —LAUREN SHULER DONNER

> "Giving people voices—
> everybody. I think that's really
> what the latter part of the
> century's about. What is the
> Internet for if not giving
> everybody a voice to say what
> they're gonna say? When
> you're building an
> organization, you're building
> intellectual capital. And the
> biggest part of that is human
> capital. That's kind of a de-
> personalized way of saying it,
> but that's what it is. When the
> sum of your company is not
> manufactured goods, real
> estate, or equipment, but
> potential, the team is
> everything, right?"
> —THOR MULLER

family call him, was also the interviewee who seemed to have thought the most about spiritual issues in business and who pressed me hardest on the use of investment metaphors for human relationships.

Mort Meyerson said, "I know that success has to do with one's ability to constructively give. People will find that by constructively giving, they will inadvertently find that they receive. It's a consequence of being open. It's not a consequence of fighting for what you think you deserve. And I think most people in business don't recognize that. They think it's 'dog eat dog.' And of course, in some companies, that's true, so it's not an illusion.

"But you can have it all. You can have good relationships. You can have win-win relationships with customers. You can share the wealth with other people. You can give things away ad infinitum, and you will find that you're better off doing that, and you will gain when it comes back.

"Now, one of the things that bothers me about what I just said is that it could be interpreted as Jesus saying, 'Cast bread upon the water and it will come back twofold.' Or Deuteronomy, where you give an unblemished sheep, and it takes care of things. That's not it. I don't really believe in gift-giving for reward.

"It's a psychological give and get. To prepare yourself to receive, you have to give. And you have to do that in relationships."

I thought about what Mort had said a lot. Had my background on Wall Street so distorted my thinking that I was simply monetizing the whole world and everything in it? I sincerely don't think so. Yes, there are things we do in the business world that are calculating, that are designed to bring us advantage, to take us to the top, to help us beat our competition, and that are done with planning and forethought. But there are also things we do that bring us pleasure, that make us feel like we are accomplishing something good for the world, that make us feel like we are touching other people, like we are having an impact, like we are sincerely bringing people into our lives in a meaningful way. This is the spiritual dimension of business—the soft stuff that incorporates people, relationships, heart.

> "There were these two companies: very similar in their goals, their technologies, their missions, everything. I knew both of these companies quite well. One of them raised three times the money that the other one did—because it had a specific person who said to people who trusted him, 'You really ought to put some money into this.' That was the only explanation for it."
> —DAVID KAISER

Realizing that these two perspectives are ultimately no more separate than your heart and your head is the most reliable, time-tested way I've found to achieve success.

If you try to say *I'm just going to do business with my heart; I'm only going to work with people for whom I have a warm glow and good feelings*—you're going to go down in flames. But, by the same token, if you try to say that you're a fighter jock, you don't need anybody, you're going to break the speed barrier

> "The goal is to surround yourself with good people. It's the key; it really is. Because if you think you can do it by yourself, well, then you're already in the soup."
> —CHRISTINA GOLD

and leave your heart at home and do it all alone, you're also going to fail.

The people I interviewed for this book incorporate heads and hearts into their business lives, and they do it without cynicism, without malice, without hesitation.

Many of them do it unconsciously: It comes to them as naturally as throwing a ball comes to an athlete.

Investing Isn't Networking by Another Name

When I first started working on this book, the principles weren't yet clear. My description of it was unformed at best, and confusing at worst. People who wanted to be supportive tried to help by saying, "Oh, so it's a book about networking." I would explain why it was *not* about networking in the common way that word is used. Eventually, I was able to explain that this book relates to classic networking the same way the graphics you download from a porn site relate to the act of marital intimacy: The actions may look similar, but the intentions and consequences couldn't be more dissimilar. You're creating a network, not networking.

If you were part of the business world in the 1980s and early '90s, you grew up with and probably believed—at least for a while—in the mantra of networking. You probably spent months of your life going to cocktail parties and industry gatherings and drink dates and lunch dates. You were probably part of one or more small, industry networking groups. You probably are still drowning in business cards.

The problem was, most of us had no clue what to do with the people once we networked with them.

We'd talk about business for a few minutes, we'd get a card, we'd make a follow-up call, maybe go on a drink date, and before long we'd have a triple-width Rolodex bursting with business cards like an October pomegranate.

Then, six months later, while we were still exhausting ourselves by going out to industry functions every night and going on business lunches every day, cramming more and more business cards into our Rolodexes—

> "Where you have a strong positive relationship with someone, that relationship will last even if the person leaves the company. Of course, their goals and priorities will change, and you must understand and work with that just as you would in any business relationship. But the basic person has not changed. I have seen people classify those who leave an organization as untrustworthy traitors rather than as potentially strong business partners. The world has to be seen as a relationship network."
>
> —JEAN HAMILTON

the cards from the people we met months back were as meaningful to us as if they had been written in ancient Greek.

When working with people and investing in relationships, the value comes not in quantity, but in quality. It doesn't matter how many people you've met in your career, or how many Rolodex cards you've acquired, or how many people you can call by name on the floor of a convention center. What matters is who will be there for you when you really need it. And what real value the relationship can bring to you.

> "**R**elationships have to do with shared mission, or passion. It's got no relation to 'networking'—which I hate and won't do. When you have a strong relationship, it's more of a sense that *'I've met my match.'*"
>
> —NANCY EVANS

Don Duckworth, Chairman and CEO of the investment and management consulting firm The CWD Group, said to me, "This concept today, this mantra of networking, is laughable. I can't tell you how many people come to me and say 'I want to network with you.' And it's clear: They've been told to network, they've been told that that's what you have to do if you want to get a better job, or get promoted, so that's what they do. It has become more about the process than the outcome.

"People need to understand that you don't just exchange business cards with someone and that gives you some relationship with them—some bond that will make them want to help you. 'Networking' is superficial. 'Relationships' are deep."

I'll Give You Two Lawyers for a CFO

When I think of another faux-personal trap that people fall into, I'm reminded of how, back when I was a girl, the boys used to collect and trade baseball cards. They would hoard as many cards as they could get their grubby little hands on, they would sort them endlessly, and strategize ways of finding the ones they were missing. This could entertain them for months on end.

Most people who learned the eighties style of networking treat their Rolodex cards the same way. These people think that their business contacts are currency that they are free to trade, barter with, negotiate for, and juggle back and forth. This somehow feels personal to them because it involves people instead of circuits, I guess, but the effect it has on relationships is, of course, chilling.

People who play this game seem to feel fine about bartering with relationships, using their relationships with people as payment in trade for other services. They gladly give out people's phone numbers and introductions as a way, they think, to widen their circle and to increase their influence. The more the merrier.

It doesn't work.

People and relationships can't be traded back and forth like real estate in a game of Monopoly. The contacts you make with people in business each have a distinct flavor and character, and each of them connects you to a living, breathing human being who gave you his business card for a reason: Because he thought he might like to hear from *you* again, not from your boss or your friend Joe or the person you just met in line at Starbucks.

For relationships to be valuable, they need to be respected, honored, and treated with the importance that they deserve. Relationships are treasured property. But the old rules of networking did nothing to honor that value. In fact, the opposite was the case: The tone of networking—indeed the very word—implied that the individual relationships were just the smallest part of a larger, growing and breathing whole in which the parts were meaningless.

If someone feels that you give his name to every Tom, Dick, and Harriet you meet in an airport first-class lounge, chances are that that person is going to feel used and is going to feel that you don't hold your relationship with him in high value. If, however, someone feels that you protect your relationship with him and never trade on it; or, in fact, if he feels that the only time you have given his name out was when you gave it to a handpicked third person who was enormously helpful to him and whom he could not have gotten to on his own; then you have done something to show how much you value your relationship.

How You Can Tell When Relationship Opportunity Knocks

One of the great relationship naturals I interviewed was Danny Meyer, proprietor of four of New York City's most successful restaurants (including his flagship Union Square Cafe, which has been voted the number one–rated restaurant in the city by Zagat for the past four years). Danny and I were sitting in the lovely upstairs room of Union Square Cafe several hours before the first customer would come in through the front doors for lunch. Service people had begun to set tables and polish silverware and get the room ready for the next meal, and we could hear the voices and the sounds of people working and chopping in the kitchen, beginning to prepare the meals for the customers that would start arriving later in the day.

While we were chatting, we heard an out-of-place tapping coming from the front of the restaurant. It was hard for me to place the sound, and we continued to talk over it, but it was clear to me that Danny had noticed the sound and was becoming preoccupied with it.

I asked one more question, and we heard the tapping sound again, and Danny finally apologized to me and left the table.

He was back in a moment, was very apologetic for having left, and told me that he knew the sound was someone tapping at the window trying to get in. "It was a repairman, here about something in the kitchen."

It was quite clear that there were enough people walking back and forth around the restaurant that someone else would have noticed the person tapping on the glass in a few moments and let him in. But that wasn't good enough for Danny.

"I know that if that repairman doesn't feel the same level of hospitality from us that our diners feel, then it will affect the quality of hospitality we will be able to offer our customers.

"It doesn't matter what he's here to fix. I want him to feel that of all the restaurants in town that need his services, he wants to come here first, because he feels that we're on his side.

"It's pretty basic stuff, but it's crucial for business. We're only as good as the weakest ingredient. We want to be a favorite account of the guy who sells us tuna. We want the best piece of tuna. That doesn't happen unless the last time he came here he felt as well cared for as someone in the dining room sitting down to grilled salmon and a glass of sauvignon blanc."

Danny answered for me one of the great strategic relationship questions: which ones matter the most. There are a lot of people out there with *the* answer to that question. You'll hear that clients matter most. Or that vendors matter most. Or your boss matters most. Or your prospects.

The home truth is that the tuna guy matters most. The tuna guy is the person you count on to help you make it happen, who is not necessarily your biggest client or your current boss. As we go on, you'll learn how to spot the tuna guy and what to do once you do.

Real Tuna Guys

Relationships are based on real human emotion, not on superficial tactics for widening your circle. A wide circle is certainly not a bad thing to have, but size isn't the only important factor. What would you rather have: a million anonymous investors with one share each guiding your company, or twelve handpicked, intelligent people whom you know and trust on your board of directors and who care about the company and really care about your success?

> "If you're the CEO, or the head of HR, or whatever, in a corporation, and you're fabulous at what you do, but you don't get out and talk to business people, and they don't trust you, and they don't come to you when they should be coming to you with important issues, then really, how good can you be? You have to rely on other people to make the company successful. You have to be able to work together. You don't have to love each other, but you do have to work together."
>
> —JULIE DAUM

The same thing goes for your career. You don't want one hundred anonymous people deciding your future for you. Instead, you want to have a few people whom you respect and who know you—your strengths, weaknesses, and potential—to guide you when you need help. **You need a personal board of directors.** These are people who, as Pat Zenner, President and CEO of Hoffmann-La Roche Inc., said, "Can coach you, give you advice, develop you, and be sounding boards for you." They are your closest business relationships. These are the people who will help you expand and grow professionally and will have your interests at heart. Everyone at any level of any organization can use a personal board of directors.

The relationships you're given, like coworkers, are no longer enough. In a world in which millions of people telecommute, in which millions own small entrepreneurial businesses, in which millions work for huge corporations but in far-flung, off-site locations, in which a career is made up of several short episodes—the relationships that you form outside of your current organization may turn out to be the most important to your ultimate success.

Repeat that: *The relationships that you form outside of your current organization may turn out to be the most important to your ultimate success.*

Even if you work for a Fortune 100 company, you know in your heart that you are a freelancer: We are each of us solely responsible for our careers and our own success, and we are the only ones who will walk our unique path through the business world. You work for what Jon Katzenbach referred to as *Me, Inc.* But that doesn't mean that you do it alone.

What do you need? What the most successful people have— the most powerful, renewable, dynamic source of business energy on earth: the right people on their side. For some, this power of personal connection might include a tight circle of intimates, for others, a broad community of well-wishers, for still others, a group of mentors. The shapes vary and change depending on the person, the career track, and the timing. But for all it is a grouping of people whose influence and intelligence create a safety net against failure, a springboard for success, and a think-tank for business strategies.

Successful people—sometimes consciously, sometimes not—

create their own personal boards of directors: groupings of other people, often with disparate backgrounds, who bring a breadth and depth of experiences, knowledge and connections. The board of directors creates for any successful person a powerful support community that works on a grander scale than any one company or any one individual could manage alone.

The personal board is the most powerful asset any businessperson can have. If you work on building strong trust-based business relationships using the nine principles I describe in this book, you'll have the knowledge and the wherewithal to create your own. And like the people you will read about in this book, your possibilities for success will be infinite.

Relationships Are Your Future

Shelly Lazarus knows that it's all about closeness, which is why she says that her entire growth strategy for Ogilvy is based on current clients. She knows that when she strengthens the relationships the company already has with clients, those clients do more business with Ogilvy; and when executives from the client companies move on to different jobs—if they had a really terrific relationship with Ogilvy—there's usually a way they can come back and work together again.

And Danny Meyer knows that unless everyone he does business with feels like an honored guest, his business will lose the magical edge it has over the rest of the New York restaurant world.

What these people know, and you will, too, is that the trick is to make it personal, to bring your heart into it, while respecting the roles and the rules of business. The goal is not to do business with your friends, and it's not to make friends out of your closest business relationships (though that sometimes happens). It's to be present, and to bring all the nuance and intensity and affection and power of your personality into your close business relationships. It's precarious, it's difficult, it brings forth your anxieties and insecurities and tests your strength as well as your faith. More on this in Principle Two.

Observe the Rules of the Role

"I think it's good to identify with your role, but at the same time you have to understand who likes you for yourself and who likes you for what you've got."

—ESTHER DYSON

BEFORE WE EMBARK ON THE RELATIONSHIP-BUILDING JOURNEY, WE need to stop and learn the role rules.

Every business relationship has a role attached, even if that role is not necessarily clear. And along with every role comes a set of expectations about how that role interacts with all the others. If you're the boss, the employee looks after your needs; if you're the client, you can make demands that might well be inappropriate otherwise; if you're an executive secretary, you look after your boss's needs, and you are particularly solicitous toward the people who are important to his career.

In a business environment, you ignore the conventions of role at your own risk. However, successful people know that there are ways to be flexible: They have an instinctive understanding that the power of relationship can far outweigh the power of the role.

ROLE RULE #1: SOMETIMES YOU HAVE TO DRIVE ON THE SHOULDER

Traditionally, in business, the person in the superior role was responsible for setting the tone for building a relationship. He called the shots, he let the people beneath him know just how much intimacy and attention he required and felt comfortable with. It was very clear to everyone whether or not you could invite the chairman out for a cup of coffee. The answer was usually "not."

But now, what was a nice neat system has become fluid. Where it used to be quite obvious to everyone that the right way to respect role was for the subordinate people to bend themselves to the relationship requirements of their superiors, it's now no longer nearly as clear. With hierarchical structures getting murky, the real power lies in a person's ability to give everyone, in all directions, what they need. And successful people understand that.

Here's a fascinating example: Southwest Airlines, which is one of the best-run companies in America, has an executive named Colleen Barrett with whom I talked at great length. Colleen has the title *Executive Vice President—Customer Service*. But here's the part I really love: At Southwest, the term *customers* includes employees. It is embedded in the very structure of the corporation that their employees are treated as if they were customers and deserve the same respect and attention.

It turns the traditional role structure on its head. Colleen is effectively treating her employees as if they were her employers. She is treating them as if they were important clients of the company, which—to Southwest—they are. That's part of what makes Southwest such an incredibly successful company, one that beats its competition by virtually any measure.

She told me, "We recognize each significant event in an employee's life that
we know about; and I spend half my
time trying to know about all of them. I
tell supervisors at every location that
they are responsible for picking up the
phone and letting me know every time
there's an important event in the lives
of one of their people, good or bad. It's
not published anywhere, but our core
value is, basically, to follow the Golden
Rule. I tell employees that when they're
dealing with our external customers
that, sure we have rules and procedures,
but when they're dealing with a situation as it's happening, they should forget

> "You don't want a role. You
> want to be a part of the family,
> to be there for everyone. But
> there are times when you
> have to play the role and be a
> disciplinarian. At the end of
> the day, on the way home,
> you're angry with yourself,
> you had to make an actor *do it
> your way*—what you as the
> director wanted for the good
> of the film. The normal venue
> didn't work, so you reverted to
> a form of Authority."
> —RICHARD DONNER

the procedures and do the right thing. Treat people the way you
want to be treated, and I just don't see how you can go wrong. It's
the way we are. It's not a program, it's not an initiative—it's what
we do every day, every way. We have titles at Southwest—I don't
think you can have a big company without titles—but we don't
think in terms of titles. And we certainly don't think in terms of
rank, or of management vs. non-management."

Southwest behaves on a corporate level the way successful people behave as individuals. Over and over what I have found is that
successful people treat people who are their subordinates as if they
are their superiors. They pay more attention than the role demands, they provide emotional support and sustenance to employees and to clients in a way that builds the relationship and
creates loyalty and affection.

Basically, they are treating employees the way employees used
to treat their bosses. They reach out, they make the first move,
they give before they receive, they pay attention. Is that sucking
up? Sometimes, if, as I do, you consider sucking up to be simply
paying attention to other people's needs. It's taking the time and

investing the energy to imagine how the other person might be feeling and what the other person's emotional needs might be and trying to connect with them on a personal level.

Successful people don't always put hierarchy first in dealing with people, and in fact they often don't think vertically at all: They simply think of where they need to go to get results. Sometimes it's people below them in the hierarchy, sometimes it's people above them. They know that positional power is not a requirement for getting the job done.

No one would expect that David Rockefeller, one of the world's richest men, would bother to invest in relationships with people who are beneath him (which, let's face it, is virtually everybody), but he is passionate about it. And he does it because he knows that relationships are what give him added ability to make a difference. (You'll learn more about how he does it in Principle Seven.)

Bernie Marcus, Chairman of Home Depot, said, "You know, when you're the CEO of a big company, you walk into a room and people are intimidated by you, by the power you have, by the role you play. So, if you're one of those people, you find that you're talking to yourself, you're pontificating because, 1) no one is going to interrupt you, and 2) no one is going to disagree with you because they're terrified of the power you have over them. So they sit there nodding their heads because they think that's what you want. When what you really want and need, of course, is for the people who work for you to talk to you as freely as they do to their coworkers. I try to go into stores and talk to people there and ask questions and be really open to what they tell me. Just this

> "I believe quantitative judgment has its place because you can measure with it, but it's a minor place. The problem with it is that once you measure things, then you can rank them, and once you rank things, you think you understand them. But in relationships, measuring and ranking means nothing because you can't measure and rank relationships. It simply doesn't work."
> —MORT MEYERSON

week I had someone tell me about something amazingly stupid we were doing in the stores, and we changed that policy right away."

Unsuccessful people, on the other hand, tend to have a very tight definition of role, and only see the world in terms of vertical relationships. They focus on whom they *have* to be nice to: They have to be nice to the big client, they don't have to be nice to the big client's secretary. They have to be nice to their boss, they don't have to be nice to the lawyer who is working for him.

They think that role allows them to be abusive, that it gives them latitude to ignore the relationship needs of anyone who doesn't require it because of their superior role. And, in the new workplace, it destines them to failure.

ROLE RULE #2: WHEN PARKING, GIVE THE OTHER GUY ROOM TO GET IN AND OUT

While successful people understand the limitation of role, they also know that it's important to respect their boundaries.

Roles come with expectations. For example, the role of most employees in a corporate structure comes with the expectation that the employees will take care of their bosses' needs and follow their bosses' directions. The role of most people who work in sales includes an expectation that they will work hard to enchant their clients by not only taking care of their business needs, but also by social niceties: taking them out to dinner, sending holiday cards, taking them out to play golf. The role of people who are bosses includes an expectation that they will solve problems and provide direction, but not necessarily that they will cater to their underling's needs.

And you can only step out of the boundaries of a role with care.

Consider this story about Paul Morgan, a crackerjack real-estate agent. He handled the sale or rental of huge tracts of office space for corporate clients, earning commissions in the hundreds of thousands of dollars.

One of his clients was a major national insurance company

whose business was growing exponentially—and, therefore, whose real estate needs were voracious. Paul's client was Grace, a veteran of the business, who handled all office services and physical plant operations for the business worldwide. She was an enormously busy woman, with a personal style that veered toward the abrupt. She knew what she wanted, when she wanted it, and she had no patience for any waste of her time or effort.

At the beginning of their relationship, Paul was returning Grace's calls within minutes—often giving up his weekends to take her around to see new possible spaces. As she learned to trust him, and gave him more and more of her business, they would occasionally go out to dinner after a day of seeing prospective office sites to discuss the relative merits of each. More and more, he understood her needs and, as she grew to trust him, their relationship grew easier.

After several years (and several million dollars' worth of real-estate transactions) and as Paul's career grew, and he became more successful, he became less and less accessible to Grace. He'd take a day or two to return her calls, he'd send an associate to show her a new space. When they would go out to dinner, he kept steering the conversation to his own business and how he was now thinking of building office parks. Grace would have to interrupt him to talk about her upcoming moves.

Paul believed that the relationship he'd developed with Grace was so strong that the requirement of his role was diminished. He was wrong. Grace moved her business to a competitor, and Paul lost 25 percent of his commissions overnight.

It's critical, when dealing with a business relationship, to be vigilant in assessing the requirements of a role, and to assume that those requirements will take precedence over a relationship. The strength of the relationship may well allow you to ignore the role requirements occasionally, but not often, and not for long. Once Paul lost his role, it was inevitable that he would lose his commissions.

Phyllis Grann, President and CEO of Penguin Putnam Inc. and arguably the most powerful woman in the book publishing business, prides herself on her strong relationship with the house's authors. And she should. She told me, "Years ago, when Lew Wasserman at MCA hired me to work at Putnam, he told me that his philosophy was: 'You're nothing without the talent.' I've never let go of that: The authors are the most important thing in our business. It's their name on the books, without them, there is no company.

"So, one of the things you do is take care of their needs. We're like the old movie studios in that way; whatever they need, we try to help them. I've gotten involved in their lives, and they are involved in mine. But I'm always conscious that there be no burden in it for them. My inclination is to always let them lead and to decrease their burden. It's my job to take care of them."

Phyllis Grann's way of getting close but respecting the role is a master class in relationship building.

ROLE RULE #3: KNOW WHAT YOU'RE DRIVING, AND IF YOU'RE DRIVING

There is a tendency these days, among certain kinds of companies (Silicon Valley leading the way), to do away with roles altogether. It's an interesting experiment, but then again, so was New Coke.

Without clear roles, you end up with companies where employees have titles like "Chief Rabble Rouser" or—as seen on an actual business card that floated past me recently—"Content Machine." There are even companies—like Hollywood's DreamWorks— where there are no titles at all.

This kind of an environment can be incredibly energizing and exciting, when it all works well and people feel they can communicate and get things done and be part of the dialogue. It seems to work best in small organizations, where everyone knows everyone else by first name and everyone knows one another's strengths and weaknesses. It is a fascinating acknowledgment of the importance of relationships in the new business paradigm.

But it also can be much more dysfunctional.

And it often just doesn't work.

If you're thinking of working in an organization that does not have defined roles, you need to make sure that your personal appetite for role definition and for structured authority will allow you to survive.

Ask yourself these basic questions:

When someone first tells you to do something, do you do it, or do you ask why?

When the boss gives you an assignment, do you try to do it his way? Or do you experiment?

Do you order off the menu?

The Godfather or *The Sopranos*?

Do you try the automated system, or demand to speak to someone on the phone?

If you have to ask how to score this test, *don't* try to work in an unstructured environment. Please.

When small entrepreneurial and start-up operations are being formed, their client base and staff begin with their friends. The environment is freestyle and emotional. Meetings are impromptu and hierarchy doesn't exist. The staff works till midnight and then goes out to dinner together. Decisions are made by consensus, meaning six people standing over the coffee machine in the hallway.

But as the businesses grow and the emotional demands become unbearable (how can you be emotionally involved with 100 people?) these organizations shift over from relationships being primary to role being primary. Suddenly the senior vice president (whether that's his given title or not) is making decisions at a formal meeting, or alone in his office and disseminating it by e-mail, when not that long ago everyone felt that they had a say. That leads to resentment, anger, and probably a much worse morale problem than if people had simply been hired with titles and knew what the positional power structure was right from the start.

Without defined roles, colleagues work in teams on equal foot-ing and are forced to use their relationship skills to get decisions made. It's a process of cajoling, of endurance, of sheer determi-nation. And it can lead to paralysis. For many people, it's just too exhausting.

ROLE RULE #4: YOU ARE NOT WHAT YOU DRIVE

Raylene Decatur, President and CEO of the Denver Museum of Nature and Science, told this story: a CEO with whom she did business had retired about two years back. A few months ago, he called her and left an unspecific message that he wanted to talk to her about something. She called him back within twenty minutes.

He said to her, "Raylene, you continue to impress me." And she asked, "Why? All I did is return a phone call." He told her: "You can't imagine how many people don't return my phone calls now that I'm no longer in that job."

The issue struck her as an important one about business rela-tionships.

"If I quit this job today, I wouldn't have one-twelfth the profile I currently have in Denver. And I have no illusions, for a great majority of relationships that I'm in, the positional power is what is important. But there are a few business relationships that would carry on, and might in fact even flourish because the strictures of the role would be gone.

"I worry that there are too many people out there in their forties whose phones are ringing off the hook and whose e-mail in-boxes are overflowing and who have people pounding on their doors— and they just can't imagine that it's all positional power and that if they leave or lose their job, it'll all be gone. Unless they work to have it be otherwise."

Money can't buy you love, but it sure can buy you something that feels like it. It can buy you status, it can buy you temporary devotion, it can buy you the attention of other people. When you're

> "One of the concerns I had when I retired almost two years ago was that now that I've given up the role of CEO of Toys 'R' Us, what will my relationships mean? How much of relationship is dependent on who you are, and how much on the position you have? By being the CEO of a big company, you automatically get a lot of power and prestige . . . and you can't help but wonder if that masks how people really feel about you. People say, when you stop having the power to write an order, or write a check, you're nothing. The amazing thing was, I didn't find that to be the case at all. The relationships continued. And when, in retirement, I began spending a lot of time on children's charities—I was able to help raise tens of millions of dollars and virtually all of it came from the relationships I had developed in business. People could have turned their backs on me: After all, instead of making them money, I was now asking them to give me money. But they didn't."
>
> —MICHAEL GOLDSTEIN

in a position of power, other people are, in effect, being paid to be nice to you. And it feels great. Jim Farrell, CEO of the Fortune 500 company Illinois Tool Works, said, "When you're a first-year CEO, you get tons of requests to go here, to speak. And it's flattering. But, of course, it's just the title and the company and the money that impresses people; you could be Bozo the Clown, CEO of Illinois Tool Works, and you'd get a lot of opportunity."

But having that sort of power misleads many people into believing that they have real relationships, when all they have is position.

I heard a story of a retired CEO who complained that, once he was out of his office, his former colleagues and business associates would never return his calls. I talked to one of his ex-employees, who told me, "You know, he treated people horribly. He was a miserable son of a bitch to all of us, but he had no awareness of that fact."

And, of course, the minute they were no longer obliged to be nice to him, they weren't.

Relationships help you to transcend your role, and successful people understand that. Ultimately, all roles are finite. Real relationships are renewable. If you want long-term transcendent success, you'll be aware and mindful of both the role and the relationship. But with key relationships, you'll pay as much attention to relationship as to role. The day comes for all of us when other people no longer feel it is a requirement of their job to take our telephone calls. That's when the true value of your relationships will shine forth: when people take your calls because they want to.

ROLE RULE #5: KEEP CHECKING THE TRAFFIC LIGHTS—THEY CAN CHANGE QUICKLY

Michael and Ellen Brooks constantly check the traffic lights. As providers of large scale video systems to such clients as Madison Square Garden, AT&T, and Lucent Technologies, they have fierce competition who would like a piece of their action. They know that while doing business with your competitors might seem like a red-light relationship, sometimes it's green.

Michael Brooks explained further how this works: "There's sort of an unwritten rule. We don't steal one another's clients. We know they know a lot about us and who our clients are, and vice versa, and we will butt heads as far as bidding for a certain job. For instance, we know that NBC is going to be looking for vendors to supply screens for the Olympics, and we already know that we're going to be one of three companies bidding on it, and we know the other two are friendly competition. So we're all going to try to do the best we can to beat the other guy out, but whoever wins, wins, and we go on with life."

But as Ellen Brooks points out, "Whoever wins will probably come to us to supplement, because now we have equipment that they need."

While they respect the role rules of competition, Ellen and Michael Brooks have found a way to make it personal and friendly. And from the Olympics story, we see how they make what could be a red-light competitive relationship a green light because they've established relationships with their competitors. They will earn money with or without the NBC contract, and they know that whoever gets the contract, it's in their best interest to maintain a cordial relationship.

ROLE RULE #6: IS YOUR CAR FOR PLEASURE OR BUSINESS?

This issue is not as basic as it looks. There often isn't a clear line between true friendships and business buddies. Even during the course of a day, the line can get pretty blurry. If the line gets too blurry, though, it means that one or both of you are creating unspoken expectations that may or may not be met. And unmet expectations, as we all know, are bad for business, worse for friendship, and most painful of all for love.

There is nothing in my business career that's left as much lingering pain as blurred business/personal relationships gone wrong. I know I'm not alone in this—of the many problems I hear about people encountering in their business lives, this kind of problem is often the most upsetting.

How to tell which is which? It's hard, and that's why the rest of this chapter is devoted to answering that question, and to telling you how to handle situations when you really have to do business with friends. Following are some rules that can help you understand how to separate the people with whom you should be making business magic, and the people with whom you shouldn't.

If you really need to figure out for yourself if a relationship is primarily business or personal, remember this cardinal rule: If making money is involved, it's business. Period. Just like any friendship between two people that leads to sex can no longer be a pure friendship (Do you doubt that? Rent the *When Harry Met Sally* . . . video again.), once the specter of money enters a relationship, it isn't a pure friendship.

Once money is an issue, power is an issue. There's no way around it. We all want money; we all need money. If there's another person in your life who can influence the amount of money you have in your pocket, he has power over you, and both you and he know it.

That person becomes the pursued—just like in a sexual relationship. And he can get caught up in playing the same power games. And, of course, this doesn't apply only to the people who sign your paycheck. They are just the most obvious and blatant example of someone whose power over your financial life skews any chance of a truly balanced friendship. This distinction also holds true for anyone who can influence others who pay you money, who can have a positive (or negative) effect on your career status, or can in any way enhance your job performance.

All of these relationships are business relationships. Never think that someone in any of these positions in your life is someone with whom you can be completely uninhibited:

- Employer

- Employee

- Client

- Coworker

- Media contact

- Lawyer

- Accountant

- Advisor

- Consultant

- Investor

You get the idea.

Now, don't get insulted. Am I saying that you can't have a warm, intimate, and satisfying relationship with anyone in your business life? Of course not. Am I saying that your relationship with them needs to be cold and cynical? No. All I'm saying is that there are issues that need to be taken into consideration when business is part of the equation that you don't need to bother with otherwise—and you ignore those issues at your own peril.

Business relationships need to be tended to and cultivated and cared for in a different way from friendships. The best answer I got to my question about how to tell the difference between friends and business relationships was from my former boss, President and CEO of Prudential Securities, Inc., Wick Simmons. Wick put it as clearly as possible: "Friends don't give a shit about what you do."

Following is a longer list of questions to help you figure out the difference.

The fact that I'm asking you to recognize the difference between business relationships and friendships is not meant to lessen or falsify those relationships. In fact, it's to help you to highlight which relationships may have an impact on your success and help you to work with them in an honest, enriching, and spiritually fulfilling way.

> "I do not go out on Saturday nights with clients. We're not personal friends. I'm not even sure that it's good that you become personal friends. Because then the clients lose a little bit of objectivity. Whereas, if the relationship is a work relationship, but a very close one, I find clients feel perfectly comfortable calling me up after the meeting and saying, 'I didn't want to say it in front of everyone, but I just don't like that. Take it away. I never want to see it again.' "
> —SHELLY LAZARUS

Before we talk more about friends, I want to talk about two other kinds of business relationships that can be as confusing as friendships.

1. Friendly, Not Friends.

These are the people you like to work with, who are nice, good people, whom you have fun with and whose company you enjoy. But you know in your heart that they're just not all that good at their jobs. You can like them, you can be friendly with them, but if you're driven to get results and to succeed, making a relationship like this too important can only harm you. It'll lead to heartache in the long run.

Bill Aldinger, Chairman and CEO of Household International, said, "You have to distinguish between *respect* and *like*. Being liked is not necessarily the right thing. You'll hear people say in the workplace, 'Gee, I think that person's won-

Think of someone with whom you have a relationship and ask yourself these questions: If the answer to any of them is yes, the person you're thinking of is someone with whom you have a business relationship and must be treated as one:

Does he pay me?

Do I hope that someday he will pay me?

Does he influence the amount of money I get paid?

Can he influence people with whom I work?

Can his connections have an impact on my success?

Do I want something from him (sex and love don't count)?

Can he open doors for me?

Can he introduce me to potential clients?

Can he help promote me or my business?

Can he harm my business?

Does he work for me?

Do I hope that someday he will work for me?

If you answered no to all of the above, great: That relationship is free and clear of business issues, and you can do with it what you damn well please, at least as far as I'm concerned.

But even one yes and you need to move that relationship in your mind firmly into column "B" for "Business" and follow the rules in this book.

derful—and I love to have them over to my house'—but when you ask if they're effective leaders, or if they would follow that person over walls, then the tone changes. Trust is based on the ability to perform. Honesty, clarity, other qualities are part of it—but performance leads the way."

2. You Don't Like 'Em, but You Trust 'Em.

I have to say that, in many ways, this isn't a bad business relationship. It's uncomplicated, you know what to expect, it moves the mission forward, there are no hidden agendas.

You go into every situation with this sort of person knowing that their biases are going to be completely different from yours. They are unlike you. Period. They act from a different set of values, a different set of beliefs. You know that if you are going to spend a Saturday night at a Hillary Clinton fund-raiser, they're home reading Rush Limbaugh. If you're at the multiplex seeing *Sense and Sensibility*, they're in the theater next door watching *Terminator 2*.

You have nothing in common.

Except the business agenda. And that's a good thing. You know what to expect because you trust them. There won't be any surprises, you know that their decisions are going to be made based on a framework that you can understand, even if you don't always agree with it. You have common ground in the particular business or organizational agenda, and in that, you can agree.

This can be a valuable business relationship, although it won't ever be your most valuable.

FRIENDS

Talking about friends and business is problematic. I learned how sensitive a subject it is the hard way. A year or so ago, I flew to Boston to give a speech to a roomful of accountants on the subject of work relationships and office politics. Speaking engagements are usually great. I walk away feeling like I've touched people, like we've all had a good time, like they've learned some things, and I've learned some things. I enjoy them.

Not this time.

I've never before had a roomful of people hate me the way that group did. There was not a smile, not a knowing nod in the room. I finished my speech, went to the reception, ran for the shuttle, and immediately offered to return my fee to the company—an offer that they graciously accepted without a moment's guilt or hesitation.

It was all because I had started off with this nugget, lifted from my first book: *Friends are what you have outside the office.*

Now, yes, I admit it: Perhaps I was being a bit impertinent and exaggerated my point. But the point is one that needs to be made and needs to be understood by anyone who wants to truly succeed. The needs of a friendship and the requirements of a role don't mesh easily, and often either one or the other have to flex so far that they break. Making them work in concert takes supreme concentration and devotion, flexibility and strength.

If you want a simplistic answer and, yes, it's truly simplistic, *you may not be able to have friends at work.* But before you slam the book down and go storming back to your neighborhood bookstore asking for your money back, let me elaborate.

> "You know what friends are to me? That you don't talk business. I don't want to think of myself as a real-estate broker. I want to be the girl from Edgewater who wants to talk about those pretty flowers, what the kids are doing, etc. I need a divide. I can't talk only about business. It ruins me."
> —BARBARA CORCORAN

There Are Friends, and Then There Are Friends . . .

True friendship is an emotionally based relationship. And the thing that makes friends really friends is the understanding that they are going to be supportive of one another *no matter what.* When you're in a real friendship, your interest is emotional, it's unencumbered; it's about love and caring and mutual enjoyment.

You choose to be friends with someone because of who they are, not how they perform.

But when you work with someone, or have any kind of business interest in common with someone, that can no longer really be the case. When I talked

> "With friends, you need to talk to them. Sometimes you just feel, 'I miss so-and-so and must see him or her.'"
> —ALAIR TOWNSEND

to Raylene Decatur, she said something that I thought was fascinating and precise: She said that her definition of a business relationship is *one in which the other person helps you with your ability to expand on your personal or organizational business mission.*

Every business relationship has attached to it an understanding that, somehow, someday, there is going to be a performance requirement. You know that each of you is going to have to *do* something in order for the mission to be propelled forward. You are going to have to succeed in the business world in a way that fits the mutual agenda. That creates expectation, sometimes anxiety, and certainly an obligation to achieve.

And while it's certainly the case that you can have that kind of business relationship with someone for whom you feel affection, caring, and even a certain kind of intimacy, the mix of performance expectation and affection creates emotional complexity. And, for most people, putting that kind of pressure on a true friendship can lead to the end of the friendship, which, for me, is one of life's biggest losses.

> "It's very hard to make business relationships into true friends. A real friend is someone you can share intimate things with."
> —MYRNA BLYTH

The potential for loss is also high when one of you has a business responsibility and the other wants it to be a friendship, because the closeness provided by someone with financial incentive to take care of you can temporarily feel even better than friendship.

Marcia Kilgore, whose Bliss Spa keeps growing faster and faster, described her experience this way: "I love the people I give facials to, they're great. It's unfortunate though, because sometimes I'd like to be more of a friend, but I can't because they're my clients. You begin to feel strange charging someone for a facial if you just had dinner with them. So you have to separate that a little bit because it always becomes awkward. You don't take money from your friends for doing them a favor. So, in the same way, you wouldn't take money from someone who really became a friend for giving them a facial. But then the time that you've allotted for making income, for the business, becomes non-producing time. And you can't do that."

It's a tightrope that is difficult to walk—but one that needs to be walked every time you want a relationship that gets to the level of friendship in a business context.

In a nutshell, the reason I sometimes tell people that you can't have friends at work is because balancing all the issues is so much harder than just being one or the other—friends or coworkers. You've got to have the energy for it.

Having said all this, there are times when you still want to take the risk. There are times when I do, and some of the friends I do business with are among my most cherished. Following are some rules to help.

Business with a Friend Rule 1: Figure Out Your Roles and Announce Them in Advance

Some people I interviewed felt that they could have friends at work if they were in positions that were not directly involved with one another. Ellen Levine, Editor-in-Chief of *Good Housekeeping*, said, "If you work directly with someone you care for, it could be a terrific friendship, but will get ruined. You don't do it. The same way most people can't travel for two weeks with a best friend."

Others believe that they can have friends at work if they work in different departments, if they're never going to be competing for the same bit of business, or for the same job. Basically, they make it work under the same rules as marriage between cousins: You have to be at a sufficient enough remove to not screw up the gene pool.

Business with a Friend Rule 2: Remind Yourself That Performance Comes First. Period.

If you are in a situation in which you are accountable for getting results for an organization—*that* needs to be your priority. To ever put relationships ahead of performance in a work environment is going to hurt you, it's going to hurt the other person. It's just plain bad. End of story.

The successful people I talked to were unanimous on that point, regardless of where they stood on the issue of whether or not you could have true friends at work. Everyone agreed: Performance comes first.

Esther Dyson, computer guru and author of *Release 2.1*, said, "You have a duty to perform. When I'm putting on a conference, my duty is to the audience. And while there may be people whose companies I've invested in who think they should get to make a presentation at my conference—or if there's someone on their staffs who thinks they'd make a great keynote speaker—I have to determine by using my own best judgment who will make the best speakers for my audience."

Even Bill Pollard, Chairman and CEO of ServiceMaster, who spoke movingly about how hard it is to take a tough stand with someone you like, said, "Sometimes there's a tension when you have to deal with lack of performance of a person who is also a close friend. Often the stronger the relationship is, the harder it is to deal with a lack of performance. I didn't have any problems with my kids when they weren't measuring up. I seemed to be able to talk to them about it. And yet, we had strong relationships and continue to do so today, as they are now adults. But in the context of a business, I think the stronger the friendship, the more difficult it is to deal with lack of performance. That doesn't mean I avoid a strong friendship relationship in business, it just means that as a leader, I have a hurdle to overcome when there is a performance issue, and I just need to discipline myself to focus on what is best in the long term for the individual and the organization. Otherwise, I have a tendency to avoid dealing with the tough issues."

When there's any question of relationship versus performance, performance must win.

Business with a Friend Rule 3: You Talk About It

The difficult issue—role requirement—must be talked about in the open, and often. Doing business with a friend means these discussions are never finished.

Make sure that if you have a close friendship at work, that the issue of role requirements is well thought out, discussed, agreed upon, and constantly monitored because of constant change. There is a real need in today's business environment to be explicit about your expectations of each other.

> "You have to be analytical and clear-minded when you deal with these things, and it's not easy. But if you don't have a conflict of interest at some point, you have a very dull life."
>
> —ESTHER DYSON

The more potential someone has to be important to you on either side—if it is a very close friendship or someone whose business role has a clear and direct impact on your own—the more important it is to frequently address where the boundaries are.

Even the fact that something is hidden must be spoken about. "I really care about you, but I can't talk to you about this really juicy thing you want to know about. Don't press."

That's what makes the requirement for mutual respect even more stringent in an office friendship than it is in an outside friendship. Office friends need to be able to trust one another, of course. But in a work environment, they must also trust that there are certain things that they will be excluded from, and in order for the friendship to survive, they must feel confident enough in the relationship to know that the friendship has not been diminished.

> "The first thing I do when people who are personal friends come to me about possible business arrangements is I talk openly about what I see as the threats to the friendship. I explore the worst: How bad could it get, and what will we do if it comes to that? You never want to get to a place where you put your loyalties at risk. So, instead, I do this thing of talking it out in advance and planning for the worst. It's risk management, it's like a prenuptial agreement."
>
> —DICK CAVANAGH

Business with a Friend Rule 4:
Don't Drive Over the White Line

Unsuccessful people run into trouble by ignoring role and relationship issues and choosing to forget the fact that in the work environment, role must be respected. I can't tell you how many unhappy people call or e-mail me with work problems and use phrases like "But I thought we were friends," or "I thought she liked me," or even "I can't work for that person because I don't like him." These are all clear signs of terminal role confusion.

Where they get out of whack is by defining the relationship by their *own* need for the relationship—and that attitude is destined to fail in any sort of human interaction. Just as you know a friend's romantic relationship is in trouble when you hear "If he really loved me, he would do what I ask," you're headed for big trouble when you start to think "if he really liked me, he'd do this for me."

> "People think the relationship at work is family. Or family replacement. Or people think the relationship at work is somebody being paternalistic toward them or taking care of them. And I think that's the dark side of the relationship thing. Where people read into relationships and mentoring as an abdication of power rather than a marriage of equals."
> —RAYLENE DECATUR

Successful people know that role rules. But they also know that relationship can win. They manage to respect both, undermine neither, and pay attention to the places where there might be friction between the two.

Business with a Friend Rule 5: Signal Before You Turn

In the course of the interviews, I talked to a fair number of people who had multiple role relationships. Husbands who worked with wives, friends who worked together, former in-laws, parents, and children.

For example, in my interview with Tom Quick, President and COO of Quick & Reilly/Fleet Securities, Inc., we talked about what it meant to switch back and forth between roles with his father, who is Chairman of Quick & Reilly.

What I realized, further in the interview, was that when Tom had his employee hat on, he spoke of his father as "the Chairman." When he didn't, it was "my father." Once I started looking for it, I realized that successful people almost always send signals, conscious or otherwise, when they want to move from one role to another.

If you're doing business with someone who's also important in your personal life, remember to signal before you change lanes.

Business with a Friend Rule 6: Just Because You Were a Great Driver Yesterday Doesn't Mean You Can Drive Today
There are days when you're going to be driving a very temperamental sports car over rough terrain in a blizzard. The best you can hope for is that these rules make it easier.

Business with a Friend Rule 7: All Business with a Friend Rules Apply to Family Outings
We have all heard and lived through stories about marriages and families that broke up because adding business to the relationship was more strain than could be handled. The friendship rules not only apply to friendship, but also apply to love and family. Whether or not they should be applied more stringently to the people you love depends on you and the people you love. For most of us, the family business relationship is like being entered into the Daytona 500 without knowing how to drive a stick shift. But a few people that I interviewed for this book were NASCAR drivers; among them was Cristina Carlino, founder and Co-CEO of philosophy, whose partner is her ex-brother-in-law. She told me, "It started on a handshake. He asked, 'How much do you have under your business?' I said, 'A little over fifty grand.' He said, 'Fine, I'll match you, shake hands, we're fifty-fifty partners.' We were both young and immature, and it was the first either one of us had of any real measure of success or notoriety. And we both were too hung up on what part of the company was mine (and what part was his). And it caused a lot of in-fighting that was very damaging to both of us. And, fortunately, we grew out of it and grew up and realized that the last two people we wanted to fight with were each other."

Cristina had the strength and flexibility to weather a conflict that could have torn apart her business and her relationship. If you're in, or are considering entering, a similar kind of relationship,

the best thing you can do is be prepared. There are lots of resources available to family businesses; go out and find them before
you need them.

Now that you know the rules, like all rules, there are times they
should be broken. But know the rule that applies to the situation
you're in before you break it, and make sure it's worth risking a
fine.

Be Fluent in Both Pink and Blue

"I know I've still got a lot of learning to do, but I have loved the female-male dynamic that we have. I think it's made the company."

—CRISTINA CARLINO

AMONG OTHER THINGS, I AM A REFORMED FUTURIST. EARLY IN MY career I used to write trend forecasts, including forecasts about the future of work. One day I was talking with one of the early, great, corporate futurists, Mort Darrow, about that very topic. He told me about a conversation he'd had with some corporate bigwigs in the early 1970s about demographic change, where he announced that the entry of women into the labor force was going to be the biggest change of the twentieth century. The guys weren't worried. The only problem they could see was training women to behave properly; that is, like them.

Lots of women agreed, me among them, and in the 1980s we

tried to adopt the male rules and all went out and bought copies of Michael Korda's *Power!* to read at lunch, being careful not to spill steak tartare on either the pages or on our big, floppy, silk bow ties.

Since I gave up those ties, I've actively followed the debate over differences between men and women in general and at work. Like everyone else, I love reading Dave Barry, Deborah Tannen, John Gray, Helen Fisher, and this week's experts on why we are so inexplicable to each other. It's just that, as interested as I've been in reading about differences, talking about them is kind of embarrassing. It feels vaguely girly and unbusinesslike, like the time I got caught by the boss reading a Danielle Steele novel on the plane when we both thought I should have been devouring the latest issue of the *Financial Times*.

So, wanting to write a book that speaks to everyone and wanting to avoid being embarrassed at best and reviled at worst, I had originally hoped to stay away from gender issues in this book. But they kept coming up in interviews. In fact, one sign that the person I was talking to was starting to relax, enjoy the interview, and trust me was that he would say what he really thought about this issue instead of what we both knew he was supposed to say.

Following is what I've learned from these interviews about differences between classic male and female styles in business relationships, how it's changed, and why it matters to you.

A story first. My husband, Jim, and I were having dinner one night with a couple of friends in the television business. I got started on the question of whether or not either of them thought there were differences in how men and women handle business relationships. Both of them thought there were, and the husband, a TV writer we'll call Stanley, told me about a meeting of his that had happened a few months before to prove the point.

A network asked him to meet with them to see if they could get him to take on a project. Three development executives—all women—came to the meeting. The first began by pitching her idea, which was for a hip, contemporary comedy series. It sounded like a terrific, if unusual, idea for the network, but sort of a strange idea for Stanley, who's best known for dark material. Before Stanley could respond, another woman pitched an idea. This was for a military story. Stanley got excited . . . he'd been thinking about something like this and thought the notion had promise. He said so.

Being the smart, sensitive, thoughtful, caring (I said he was a friend, didn't I?) guy he is, he then looked over and realized that the first woman was wilting. Every bit of her body language announced: "Don't you even want to hear more about my idea?" So he quickly went back to her idea, praised it, and then listened just as enthusiastically as the third person went ahead and presented yet another idea.

Now, this didn't sound so unusual to me, so I asked him what would have happened if he had been meeting with three guys. He said, "If it had been three guys, they would have decided in advance which idea to pitch first, then second, then third. If I liked the first one, they would have stopped with that." In other words, the primary goal wouldn't have been connecting with him, it would have been each individual just getting him to agree on an idea.

In conducting the interviews for this book, I spoke with both successful men and women. Early on, after this issue surfaced with a lot of the women I interviewed, I decided to probe more with the guys. Who better to start with than Leigh Steinberg, the legendary sports agent? He has the ultimate guy fantasy job, and he spends his days dealing with guys who are, well, really, really, really guylike. Being a confident man, Leigh Steinberg was willing to talk about gender stuff, too.

"I think there is a distinct gender difference in approaching many situations. Men pride themselves on the ability to get the deal done. And I think women have a better capacity—and we're generalizing here—to think through cooperative efforts. A male will look at his role in the situation and how he individually achieved or got his goals." What I understood from Stanley and

Leigh Steinberg was that there were situations where they understood that some of the women they encountered were playing by different rules and that if they wanted to win, they had to
play differently, too. It seemed right to me, and not all that difficult. After all, I'd been working with men for a very long time
and thought I'd made all the style adaptations I was ever going
to need.

Then one of my interviews for this book taught me how wrong
I was in that assumption.

When I walked out of the elevator and approached the receptionist at the offices of one of San Francisco's oldest and most
prestigious big-deal private banks, where I was scheduled to interview the chairman, I was already feeling intimidated. The offices were grand and perfectly appointed: mahogany and leather
and red velvet and fine art all simply but boldly announcing that
this was a place of status, of money, and of old WASP guys.

After I was announced, I sank into one of the enormous leather
couches and picked up a copy of a magazine that was lying on the
polished wood end table. I thumbed through it for a minute before
stumbling across an article about . . . the chairman. It went on and
on about his vision and what a superstar investor he was. I was
feeling more awed and intimidated by the moment.

Then I was escorted into his office, which was huge, with a
sweeping view of the Bay. And sitting there, at his desk, was the
man himself. He was very trim and fit, and otherwise unremark-
able looking except for the most arresting, sparkling, pale eyes.

When we started talking, I felt more and more uneasy: He was
polite, and in his very professional way he answered every question
I put to him. He was trying to be helpful, but I got the sense that
talking about relationships, which for many people is a little too
touchy-feely, was about to make him break out in hives. He was
courteous, but also careful and clearly hoping to wrap things up
as quickly as possible.

So, of course, I began to believe that this rushed interview was
all my fault: I hadn't set up the interview well enough; I hadn't
introduced the topic clearly enough or asked the right questions.

He didn't like me, and it was all my fault. So I decided to just make as graceful an exit as possible and leave him to the rest of his day. In order to make conversation while I packed things up, I started to talk about some of the other things I was doing and had done. I mentioned some of the corporate jobs I'd had, columns I was doing, clients we had in common. I saw this click for him, and he really looked at me for the first time. He reevaluated me completely and the discussion took a completely different turn. He started to take me seriously.

I stayed for almost another hour. By the end, he'd raised the possibility of working together in the future.

I left happy, but confused. What had flipped the switch? What had suddenly made it work?

The next day I called my friend Tank to help me figure it out. I needed to know exactly what had gone wrong at the beginning of that interview or I was doomed to spend the next year of my life in interview hell. Tank patiently explained that men like to hear about credentials first. Then they can anticipate performance and know whom they can count on, which for many men has meant the difference between life and death. "Ronna," Tank said patiently, "that's why uniforms have stripes. Men like being able to read performance clearly. When you don't present credentials during an introduction, it makes us anxious."

Oh.

Belatedly, I remembered the conversation I'd had with Barbara Corcoran, one of the most powerful and successful executives in New York City real estate. She started the business in 1973 with a one-thousand-dollar investment, and now her business generates over two billion dollars in sales each year, and she employs over 500 brokers.

> "I think maybe for men, trust and confidence is another euphemism for relationship."
> —CYNTHIA METZLER

Barbara talked to me about how men introduce themselves to one another—by immediately announcing their career and position and asking for the same in return ("Hi, Jim Smith, Senior Vice President of Corporate Finance at Microsoft. And you are?") She said, "I think to myself, how rude! They're sizing each other up. A woman would never do that. A woman would play coy for two hours on what she did. Or wouldn't ask. She'd go home knowing everything about the person she'd met except for what they do."

It was comforting to understand that I wasn't alone in experiencing style difference disturbances.

> "Guys want to put everybody in their hierarchical place. Like, should I have more respect for you or are you somebody that's south of me?"
> —PAUL BIONDI

But comfort wasn't what I needed. I knew in my very bone marrow that if I couldn't find a way to shift quickly and easily between male and female relationship styles, I'd potentially have the same problem I had learning to drive a stick shift—much gear grinding and some really expensive damage.

IN THE BEGINNING, THERE WAS BLUE

You know the old saw about how fish in an aquarium don't experience water? The water isn't separate from them, or for them. Same thing with classic male relationship rules in business.

For decades, if not centuries, there was a classic model of the way men and women worked together: Either the men went into the office and the women stayed home, or the relationship operated the way my parents worked together at the D & G. My dad was in charge of things like portion control, finances, security, and purchasing; Mom kept the customers happy and solved problems with the staff. The guys would worry about the hard stuff: the money, the physical plant, the inventory. The women, the soft stuff: the customers, the staff, the complaints.

Hard was good. Soft was bad. Numbers were hard. People were soft.

One of the reasons this worked so well is that while the men did the dirty work at the office and forged forth with the classic male stuff—the building, the number crunching—they turned to their secretaries and their wives to keep connected and to answer the tricky relationship questions. In fact, secretaries were like office wives in that they often took on the task of creating and nurturing connections.

Wives arranged the out-of-office encounters: the dinner parties, the picnics, the personal vacations with business associates. And it was the wives who took the initiative to form personal bonds that went deeper than the stuff the men could forge over the conference tables.

They gave their husbands the piece of the puzzle that many of them lacked in relationship abilities. In the classic "organization man" structure, the corporate wife would answer the questions the clueless man had about relationship issues: whom to trust, whom to promote, whom to form alliances with, whom to avoid. The men would bring the relationship issues home, talk about the who-said-what-to-whom, and the wives would guide them through it—the CEO's version of a therapist.

Executives felt it, and it was true: Meeting the corporate wife was more important than any job interview or board meeting.

After the dinner parties were over, the wife would tell her husband all the relationship issues that he had probably missed: who got along well with whom, where the tension was, who she didn't feel was trustworthy, who she thought was the star. Her insights, whether right or wrong, were going to carry a lot of weight with her husband. He was going to start looking at you differently, seeing things from a new angle, perhaps even making major personnel decisions, based on the personal and relationship instincts of his wife.

For a lot of men, this still holds true—several of my male interviewees said their chief relationship counsel is their wife.

> "Women are the same as men in business relationships, totally the same. I don't regard them as different at all; I'm an early feminist in that way. I've never found any difference. Except women *are* a touch smarter and savvier. They seem to have an instinctive wisdom—about people, particularly. I've found that wives of business executives are smarter about the associates of their husbands than the husbands themselves."
> —DAVID BROWN

Both Sides Now

What's changed?

In the old days, the classic female model—what I'll call the pink model—was valued, but not explicitly or financially. Because we didn't understand the value of the relationship in the market, we didn't knowingly pay for it, or at least not highly.

Now, though, we are beginning to understand that although the classic male relationship rules of business—the blue style—is often powerful and effective, its complement—the pink style—is just as powerful and sometimes more effective.

Explicitly understanding, valuing, and mastering these differences is essential to doing well in business today.

Let's take a look at both sets of rules, for starters.

True Blue Relationship Rules

1. Feelings are not discussed, especially hurt feelings.

2. Personal items are not addressed until the end of a conversation, if ever.

3. Unsolicited feedback, particularly about appearance, is not appreciated.

4. The most satisfying discussions are about how to best accomplish a task.

5. First meetings start with a mutual recitation of accomplishments.

6. Expressions of vulnerability are bad.

7. Respect always goes to the role, not the individual.

8. Group communications reflect vertical order: It matters who is "above" and who is "below."

9. There is concern about the potential for injured egos or honor and the negative consequences of same.

10. Team goals automatically trump any individual needs, particularly emotional ones.

Pink Business Relationship Rules

1. It's important to know the person you are doing business with as a person.

2. It's your problem if you hurt a business associate's feelings.

3. The role a person has doesn't mean they're right.

4. Bonding over vulnerability is powerful.

5. In meetings, it's good to talk about personal stuff before you get down to business.

6. The time it takes to reach a consensus pays off.

7. Announcing accomplishments is self-promotion and mildly distasteful.

8. Cultivating a relationship with someone simply because they are "above" you in the chain is not highly regarded.

9. Talking about feelings is good.

10. The team matters, but it isn't all that matters.

WHAT IS PINK AND BLUE TO YOU?

So, why is this vital, anyway? Did you read the list and think either "I am true blue, proud of it and never want to waste a single second of my business life on personal nonsense," or "My feelings do matter to me and I don't understand why other people can't just be more sensitive"?

Here's why it is so important: **Half of your business world may have a different relationship style than you do**. Are you really willing to give up in advance any chance of the value that better connection with the other half could bring? I doubt it.

Am I Blue?

Being someone who wants to succeed, I suspect you want to know what to do about these differences, other than bemoan them. Following are six tips.

1. *Identify your primary style color.* Take a look at the pink and blue lists again. As you go through the list, put a true by every statement with which you agree. Compare the lists and see which one dominates. (If you don't agree with any of the statements, e-mail me. We will either exchange feelings about it if you are pink or have a shouting match and like each other better when we're done if you are blue.) Don't assume that just because you are a woman, you are pink, or because you are a man, you are blue. (Yes, my husband told me any guy in his right mind would reject the idea of a pink style. But before you reject it, try to think about how pink may help you. Live with the notion of stripes for a moment. You may get used to it, and like my very blue friend, aptly named Dan Pink, you may find it to be occasionally useful.)

A former speech writer for Al Gore, Dan Pink was trying to come up with new marketing ideas for his latest book and thought he needed to look at the situation from a different perspective— a very pink approach. So, he went out and purchased all sorts of magazines that he'd never otherwise read, including *Cosmopolitan* and a cake-decorating

> "I read somewhere that in the workplace, women will always be the ones to say, 'How was your weekend?' and all that kind of stuff, whereas men will just say, 'Do you have the file on . . . ?' I always laugh about that because, according to that theory, I'm the man. I don't go around asking every single person, 'How was your weekend?' because if I did, the day would be over before I knew it. So as it turns out, the first thing I say is usually something like, 'Put your hair in a ponytail. Oh, and hi, by the way.' I forget, because I'm focused on performance."
> —MARCIA KILGORE

magazine. And as he was reading an article about customized cakes in the cake-decorating magazine, he came up with a book promotion plan. Now, the plan was about a specific task, as befits an emphasis on blue. But he wouldn't have had the idea if he hadn't been willing to don at least a momentary pink stripe.

As Ellen Levine said: "I think it can be culture shock for a man to move from an all-male or mostly male environment to work in a mostly female environment. I know it's happened to a lot of men who have come to work here. They're shocked when you comment on their tie, or that they've gotten a haircut.

"They may have worked someplace else for ten years and never have had anyone make a comment with a personal bent."

2. *Concentrate on getting cues to the other person's style as early as possible.* Often you can tell from the way they introduce themselves. A while back I attended a big conference called Women & Co. at the luxurious Breakers Hotel in Florida. This is a yearly conference for hundreds of female CEOs to meet, build new relationships, and talk. On the first night, I was sitting at a round table and the woman to my left immediately introduced herself to me. In the time that it took to shake my hand, she told me her name, her title, the size of her company, and her company's revenues for the previous year. If I were a seriously pink person, I might have found this offensive. Fortunately, because by now I'd learned to accommodate blue styles, I knew she wasn't being cold or condescending, it was just her way of doing business. So I rattled off my credentials, too. She relaxed, and we had a good conversation.

Later that night, the woman on my right introduced herself, too. She introduced herself by first name only and began talking to me about hormone replacement therapy. Now, this woman was clearly a pink-style person. I knew not to push her for her profile and was happy to chat with her about hormones. I didn't worry. I knew we would eventually get to business, and I would learn her last name and what company she worked for. I did. Cues to style help you know what to introduce when—and why not reorder your requests if hearing it in a different order helps someone say yes?

3. *Keep your color, but add dots.* Your style is your natural strength and you want to develop it and work it. It's like your mother tongue: You will always be faster and more comprehensive in it than in any second language, particularly one you pick up as an adult.

But in the same way that picking up another language dramatically increases your ability to do business in another country, developing flexibility in the other style will do the same. Consider how powerful a deep blue is who can also manage a pink moment (think Bruce Willis in *The Sixth Sense*), or the reverse (think Goldie Hawn negotiating a tough deal).

As Mort Meyerson told me, "I think males are getting a little more room to be human, and I think females are given a little more room to be competitive." Don Stewart, President and CEO of the Chicago Community Trust, pointed out that politicians are harbingers of the same trend. He said, "I think one of the best things Bill Clinton has done in his troubled presidency is legitimize hugging. I don't know if it's an age of androgyny or what, but men, because of the female push in America, have embraced values that my father's era would have considered feminine."

4. *When you are dealing with a style of a different color, check in twice as often to see if you are really communicating.* Conversations across styles are more likely to get garbled in transmission. "No" to a pink may sound like "You hate me." "No" from a pink may sound to a blue like "Maybe later." The easiest way is to simply restate what you think you've heard, as in: "Let me say what I think you just told me. You said that we can get this done, but you have several issues to resolve first, including x, y, and z."

5. *Team up with opposites.* Several of my interviewees have simply reinvented the traditional model for this millennium. As I had

mentioned earlier, in the old days, the classic male model was seen as superior and the complement to that was valued, but often not openly, actively, or highly. Today's most successful people look for their complement, and when they find it, realize the combined value can be exponentially higher.

6. *Leave conversion efforts to missionaries.* It is tempting to try to convince other people to do it your way. For the last couple of decades, lots of people have made very nice livings trying to teach women in business how to be like men. (I haven't yet seen a book for men titled *Winning Tips for Men From Post-Menopausal CEOs,* but who knows? The world keeps on surprising me.) My experience, though, and what I've learned from the interviewees, is that the more you try to force a blue to behave like a pink, or vice versa, the more recalcitrant he or she is likely to get.

> "I could make a really good argument for the male-female CEO business model. Although I have often said I don't think there's anybody harder to work for than a woman, female insight and intuition are a critical component to any business. Men, on the other hand, have innate warrior skills that are equally important in the business jungle."
> —CRISTINA CARLINO

Consider this story:

Greg Simmons works in the telecommunications industry, running a small department of field reps and telephone sales people who try to sell combination telephone and Internet services in a local market in New England. Status is important to him: He makes sure that he, and no one else on his team, picks up the check when entertaining clients. And he is a firm believer in the corporate hierarchy: He does what his boss tells him to do; he expects the people who report to him to do what he tells them to do.

Joanna Berkley is a colleague of his who runs the creative department. Before she went into the on-line business she wrote one-act plays, two of which were produced in a forty-seat theater in New Haven, Connecticut.

They both report to the regional director of the company, and their work functions overlap. He brings in clients, she has to work with them to give them what they want. If she doesn't please them, he loses the account; if he doesn't bring them in, she's got no billings. They share P&L responsibility and an extreme distaste for the other's style.

One day, Greg, a classic blue, invited Joanna to go with him to a divisional meeting. It was a two-hour drive. Joanna wanted to talk about the boss and about "issues." Greg wanted her to leave him alone.

By the time they got to Boston, each had a laundry list of complaints. Joanna wanted to work those out, too, by confronting Greg with opportunities for improvement.

Greg let his group know that Joanna would have to learn how to be a team player and wondered aloud, repeatedly, how a great soccer player like Joanna still didn't get the rules of play.

Greg is not going to make Joanna a blue, and Joanna is not going to get Greg to think pink. And everyone around them knows it and is worse off for every day the two of them waste on conversion instead of celebration. Differences in style as profound as theirs can often produce tremendous value.

VIVE LA DIFFERENCE

A friend of mine told me something she had heard at a training conference for women. The speaker asked the group: "What do you think is the biggest mistake that women make when they negotiate?"

The women in the audience threw out lots of ideas and the speaker finally cut them off and said, "No. The biggest mistake women make when they negotiate is that they're afraid to ask for what they want for fear of damaging the relationship."

I think that statement is both right and wrong. It's wrong in that it's not a mistake to consider carefully the value of a relationship as a significant factor in making a business deal. It also assumes that the classically female style—what I've called the pink style—is a liability.

It's right in that some women get confused about *how much* the relationship matters in a given negotiation.

The truth is, the calculation needs to be much more sophisticated than that. The pink desire to preserve relationship is not a liability; in fact, as the people I've interviewed for this book attest, it's a key to business success. Why in the world should women and men not take advantage of an innate ability to build strong relationships and add value in that way?

The strength and power and value of building relationships is no longer something that anyone—male or female—can devalue. Just as Marcia Kilgore and Mort Meyerson pointed out, focusing on performance is obviously not just for men.

If you're blue, the risk is that you will put emphasis on task at the expense of relationship. If you're pink, the risk is that you will put emphasis on relationship at the expense of task.

If the process of writing this book made anything clear to me, it's that the most macho guys I could find are strong enough to choose to incorporate some pink into their blue styles and the pinkest ladies have adopted some blue.

If you want to play at the top of the game, you'll put both pink and blue in your life, too.

PRINCIPLE 4

Choose Your People Like You Choose Your Stocks

"Everybody wants to give me their business plan. They tell me that this is a great idea. I tell them I'm not interested in their business plan. I say, 'Tell me about yourself.' And I find that most people don't want to do that. They're more comfortable with some computer slide show that they've done. And I'm much more interested in how they got where they are, what kind of person they are, do we share the same values? What are they trying to accomplish?"

—MORT MEYERSON

OF COURSE, RELATIONSHIP BUILDING IS NOT AS SIMPLE AS STYLE. Knowing how to choose the right people is essential to being successful—from finding the right assistant to selecting your company's new senior vice president. While this chapter discusses themes that can and should be applied in all business relationships, the tools laid out here are particularly important for establishing your personal board of directors, which can make the difference between careers that soar and careers that slide.

Anyone can find a circle of people to surround themselves with, and anyone can manage to find ways to deepen those relationships. But if you haven't picked the right people with the right spark to share your dream with, it's like trying to bake a soufflé without the correct number of egg whites. The damned thing just won't rise.

If your work life is like most, you deal with a huge number of people—there are probably hundreds, maybe thousands, that you come into regular contact with in the course of a year. There are so many to choose from that you couldn't possibly form real relationships with even a fraction of the people you encounter every day.

What you have to do, and what most of us do without thinking, is to select. To find the value. To choose the people in whom you see a big return. To invest wisely.

> "The genuine approach to building relationships will open doors over time. I think the phony approach will not. There are those that we call the Zorros. They come in, they make their sign and they leave a mark, and they're gone. They disappear."
>
> —STEVE SIEGEL

It sounds cold and calculating, and as I mentioned earlier, Mort Meyerson completely disagreed: "Relationships are about sharing and about giving, not about winning. People are not holdings. People are not tangible. People are not quantitative. You're going to start people off on the wrong track." He's got a good point. But to my way of thinking, you still have to deal with a simple truth: You don't have enough time to forge real and intense relationships with everybody. Consciously or unconsciously, you make choices, and those choices could be the ones that will mean the difference between success and failure. But unlike investing in stocks, looking for value in relationships doesn't mean looking for money: It means looking for the people with whom you can share your dream. That said, if you have a terrific group of people on your board, they will help you achieve your dreams, which may in turn help you make money.

Jim Farrell made this analogy: "Take a look at any church, any synagogue, any group of people in which money needs to be raised from a congregation. It always turns out that twenty or thirty percent of the people give eighty percent of the money. And people always say, 'But if everyone would only give one dollar, we'd be so well off.' But that doesn't happen. In fifty, a hundred, a thousand years of history—that doesn't happen.

"The same is true in business. You have to focus on the twenty percent that you know will come through for you. If you spread your focus over the other eighty percent, you'll never make it, you'll never have the time to pay the proper attention to the twenty percent who you know you can count on."

THE BOARD

As I mentioned in the introduction, all of the successful people I spoke to have a personal board of directors, although they may not call it that. These are the people who are honest with them, have their interests (not just their company's) at heart, and help them to make better business decisions.

One of the clearest signs that someone is thinking about his or her career the wrong way is when they tell me all they really need is a mentor. It's an urban fairy tale—that somewhere out there is that special someone, a mentor, who will take over your career and then not only guide you through it, but hack through the jungle ahead of you, machete in hand, to make space for you to grow, and then in a final burst of energy, whip out a magic wand and grant you not just the job you've always wanted but a bulletproof vest to protect you from the flak that's

> "Having your own personal board of directors who actively seek out people who can coach you, give you advice, develop you, and be sounding boards for you is a very wise idea for anyone at any level of the organization."
> —PAT ZENNER

going to be flying at you once you get it. Oh, and because the mentor is doing all this selflessly, the mentor expects nothing in return, except the deep, quiet satisfaction of knowing that you got what you truly deserved. Maybe. Then again, maybe you could be waiting for this mentor a very long time.

It's not that I don't believe in mentors—I've had some great ones. In fact, I still do—they're everywhere. That's because my definition of what a great mentor does is listen and then tell you the truth about what you might need to do differently. As I think back on my mentors, what comes back are the stray moments. Things like giving Bill Tremayne a report I thought was brilliant and receiving it back covered with tiny, tiny red pencil marks; reminding me that brilliance can be obscured by typos. Honest feedback is mentoring. That's what strong, successful people look for on their board and what you should be looking for, too.

When you're building your own board, the key isn't mentoring. It's mutuality.

CEOs and boards have mutual interests. Directors don't serve unless there is something that binds them to the organization. It is a given that directors are well-respected for their achievements. Beyond that, there has to be something about them and their achievements that relates to the business. The same thing goes for you and your board.

This concept of mutuality is absolutely key to putting together your own board. Like a lot of other senior managers, I've had more than my share of folks coming to me and saying, "Would you be my mentor?" When it is clear, as it sometimes is, that what they really are asking is if I would take care of them, spend enormous amounts of energy on them, and never even get pleasure from their company because there is no chemistry between us, my internal question is: "Why would I?" Crabby? Sure. Selfish? Yes. But true? Absolutely.

It turns out that I'm not the only one who feels that way. Having talked to several of my interviewees about failed efforts to build mentoring programs in their companies, it seems one of the key reasons is the inability to provide real incentives to the mentors.

You need to know and remain conscious of why someone would be on your board. You need to work actively to make being involved in your career rewarding for them, too.

Board Selection

But which are the good choices and which are the bad choices? Are there specific traits or qualities that make people the right ones for you? How do you recognize the people whom you should take along for the ride?

This is probably one of the hardest questions you will face when shaping your career. The people you choose to bring into your circle are the people who will define you: who will broaden you or will limit you, who will engage you or will exhaust you, who will ignite your passions or suffocate them. Deciding, consciously deciding whom to involve in your business life, may be the most important career strategy decision you'll ever make. Which leads to the question, How best to decide?

In the interviews, I probed hard on this question: What do you look for? As you were coming up in your careers, who were the people you reached out to? Do you have something you'd consider a personal board? How do you find your board members?

The first thing I discovered, which was quite a surprise for me, is one thing they certainly did *not* look for. Never, in my dozens of intense interviews, did I hear a successful person tell me that they looked for someone who was more important than they were—someone already wealthy and accomplished.

I had assumed going into these interviews that people who were good at relationships and successful in business got that way, at least in part, by seeking out people who were more successful than they—people who could help them along the way. Mentors, or on Wall Street, what we called rabbis.

In fact, as I went on talking to more and more successful people, and still never heard anyone tell me that they pursued people more important than they, I began to wonder if I was just asking the wrong question. Maybe they didn't need to look for important people now that *they* were so successful. Maybe they were simply beyond that; they didn't need it anymore. Or, maybe they just weren't admitting it because, no matter how one puts it, it could be a little embarrassing.

The truth is that even when these people were starting out and still a long way from anyone's definition of success, what they looked for in people was not money, was not power, was not influence.

What they looked for were things much more closely aligned to agendas, values, and dreams. They seemed to ask themselves; is this person on the same path as me?

Thor Muller, who is CEO of Trapezo and a veteran of several start-ups in Silicon Valley, said to me that when he hires someone for one of his start-up companies, "they're buying into my dream. We have to believe in the same things. And my ability to have faith in myself allows them to have faith in themselves and in what we are doing.

"Whenever you buy anything, what you're buying is a promise: a promise of a better life, of reaching your potential—and that's particularly true when you 'buy' into a new job. The promise isn't really money. It's achievement, or acceptance . . . It's a belief that you're going to reach a new level of self-realization. You've got to be able to share the dream, or it's hopeless."

Listen and Learn

How do successful people find one another?

They listen. Mort Meyerson told me, "I listen for multitudinous things that they tell me about themselves. And then I put that against a grid and say, 'I wonder what kind of person they are based on that?' Because if you ask a person what kind of person they are, you're never going to get the right answer. They're going to tell you what they think you want to hear. So I just listen, listen real hard.

"I did some work with a consultant at Grove Systems when I was there. And at a seminar with about fifty people, he said, 'It's very important where you listen from.'"

Phyllis Grann told me a wonderful story about a publicist at her company who listened. "Elizabeth Taylor once came back from Rome, and all we were doing was putting her up in the Plaza Athenee and moving her back to her house. She called our director of PR and said, 'Marilyn, I have fifty-two trunks.' And I knew Marilyn Ducksworth was fabulous when she said, 'Fine, I'm going to call a trucking service to get them to the plane.' What Marilyn heard was not just that Elizabeth Taylor had fifty-two trunks, but also the question, 'Will you take care of me?' This might have been above and beyond the call of duty for the company, but Marilyn recognized that by doing this, she could establish trust with Elizabeth Taylor and deepen the relationship between Ms. Taylor and the company."

> "I do two or three little business schools a year, and I go around and speak to the students, and I say, 'The one thing they don't teach you in business school, which they really have to teach you, is communication, the skill of communication.' They teach you how to look at the numbers, to digest the numbers, to play the numbers, to look at strategies, to play the strategies, but they don't ever talk to you about how to listen and how to communicate with people, and I think that's the most important thing in business today."
>
> —BERNIE MARCUS

Hollywood Producer Lauren Shuler Donner echoes Phyllis Grann's experience with Liz Taylor and Marilyn. She points out that if you listen to your client or star's needs, she'll be able to do her job better.

"The best way to treat a star mostly is to just be honest and be yourself, and give them star treatment. Basically I'll give them anything they want within reason because it will make them happier; a happier actor makes it easier for the director to get a good performance from them and a good performance means a better movie. So if they want their hairdresser, they want their trailer, they want their nanny, fine,

> "You can't get to where you can listen to other people, really listen to them as individuals, until you give yourself the right to be who you are."
>
> —CHRISTINA GOLD

whatever they want within reason. Make them secure; most actors are fraught with insecurities.

"For example, there's a problem in the makeup room, they don't like their hair or makeup. Why? Because there's a tough scene that day and the actor is having a hard time with it. She doesn't like her wardrobe, why? Because *they're* insecure about their role or insecure about that scene. It all comes out of insecurity and anything you can do to help make that actor feel more secure in what they do will ultimately give you a better performance. They'll feel more comfortable to take risks and perform their role better."

Listening to someone as if they're a star will allow you, like Lauren Shuler Donner, to hear more than what is just said. And this will not only help you get a job more effectively accomplished, but also find people with common goals and dreams, which is whom you need and want on your board of directors.

What Mort Meyerson is talking about is not just listening, but using his listening skills. Jim Farrell told me, "If you're listening well, then you ought to be able to ask questions such as 'What do you mean by that?' or 'How does that work?' or 'Why is that?' It helps get the story out. I don't think many people are very good storytellers or explainers of situations. So there's got to be a give and take in order to get as much of the meaning out of the listening as possible. You have to help them tell you." Listening skills, like a good fiber optic line, can clear up the conversation. They give you the information you really need to know about a person. Following is what you should tune in to hear.

"So how in conversations can you find out whether or not someone is on your wavelength on that issue? I guess it's looking in their eyes, the earnestness with which they approach the subject. It's not scientific. Seeing how they conduct their lives, what's important to them about their positions. Are they concerned about the perks? The size of the office? How many country club memberships will I get? Instead of, what is it I'm doing or who will I be working with?"
—JEFF MAURER

Listen for patterns in their stories. Notice what stories they're choosing to tell. What are they about? I had a temp for a while who had previously worked for a lot of famous people. He constantly told me stories about how awful these people really were, how they didn't appreciate him and that every relationship with one of these person-

> "At a very early age, I learned to listen, after I watched a whole group respond to me negatively when I didn't."
> —BOB ANNUNZIATA

alities had ended on a disastrous note, after which he would stomp out. I started wondering about my situation with him and if there was any possibility our story would have a happier ending. As it became clear that it wouldn't and that we were headed toward the ultimate stomp, I decided to let him go nicely, which made it possible for us to have a relatively happy ending.

Listen for why they are the hero in their story. Everyone is the hero in their own story, so ask yourself, What is it they think makes them a hero? My assistant clearly thought of himself as a Joan of Arc type martyr. Someone else may tell me a story about how much money she made on a deal. That person thinks of herself as a hero because she can make money. Another person may discuss how awful air travel is, but the reason he's complaining is that he needed to be home to take his seven-year-old to soccer practice, which reveals a different kind of hero.

> "Kids are great litmus tests. They know when someone's listening to them or paying attention. And it's obvious to them. They get that vibe or that feeling of whether or not the adult is interested in listening to them or not. You can't fool them. So I think one of the ways to practice people skills is to talk to kids."
> —JIM FARRELL

Listen for the pronouns they use. Successful people rarely use "I." They say "we," particularly when talking about failures.

Listen to see if they're listening. The chairman of The Seagram Company Ltd., Edgar Bronfman, Sr., said to me, "Listening is something that most people aren't very good at." He's right. How frustrating is it when you're talking to somebody at a party and two minutes into the conversation, he's looking around the room to find the next person to chat with? You wonder if he even listened to your name. Edgar Bronfman said that he learned to listen when he became involved with charities. "Those people aren't employees. They're volunteers, and when they say something, you'd better listen, because otherwise they're not going to be there."

> "It doesn't take a lot more time to listen than it does to say no. Rewarding opportunities sometimes arise because you gave fifteen minutes of your time to somebody."
>
> —THOMAS QUICK

Listen to the order of what someone covers in a conversation. Did he talk about his family or his cigars first? Look for the overall sequence of the topics that they've introduced to get a sense of their priorities.

Listening trumps seeing. Dr. Harold Freeman, who has been with Harlem Hospital Center since 1967, and is also President and CEO of North General Hospital in Harlem, is one of the most accomplished men I've ever met. As someone from the corporate world, I listened in awe to his ability to turn limited organizational resources into capabilities that made life better for an entire community.

We talked a lot about perception and the degree to which we are all helplessly trapped by our own. He told me, "People look at other people through a lens . . . it could be race, it could be sex . . . it could be many things. They want to be fair. But then they look through the lens of theirs and make assumptions about people that are not true based on how they see them and not how they are." To put it another way, remember that your eye is much more likely to mislead you about a person's agenda than your ear. That person with the pink hair, crop top and multiple body piercings may in fact be a spectacular CEO.

Finally, listen to your body. Notice how you feel while you're talking to someone new in your business life. Is he invading your space? Do you feel relaxed or tense?

Most of us have kicked ourselves more than once for not listening to our "gut." Even so, it's easy to push away a gut feeling because a gut feeling can be a very small and fleeting awareness in the middle of a very busy day, full of seemingly endless, more pressing, louder concerns.

It's not smart to brush away gut feelings, though, because the information that we get from our physical selves is quite sophisticated. Why else would most people prefer meeting face to face for important deals? Because they know what all of us know, that when you are physically close to someone, you can tell a lot about them: if they are covered in nervous sweat, if their hands are dry or moist, if they have a small tic, if they are blinking rapidly, or if they are breathing shallowly or quickly. Unconsciously, we all take in information, process it, and sum it up in those tiny gut feelings.

My experience is that what you learn from listening to your body is whether or not you need to pay more conscious attention. Your gut may say, "Don't trust that guy," and it may or may not be right. Unless you are strongly intuitive and have learned to always rely on your intuition, you will need to back your gut feeling up with homework that is done by the brain.

After you get used to paying more attention to gut feelings, you can learn to get additional information through your physical senses. It helps if you learn your body's specific responses to stress: For example, I tend to respond to stress by craving sweets. One of the first signs I have that someone is somehow stressing me out is if being with them makes me crave chocolate—at 9 A.M.

SHARED AGENDAS

It might seem obvious, but the first thing that successful people look for in relationships is people who share their business agenda—be it a small agenda like getting a proposal done or a larger one like closing a deal.

Raylene Decatur told me that, sure, she could have lunch every day of the week with people who are curators, or heads of other museums, or collectors, but to her, those relationships are personal, not business. Yes, there are shared issues, but not shared agendas. When you and the other person each have something to gain, each have something—usually money—to potentially make or lose, then there is a shared agenda.

Bob Annunziata, Chairman of PF.Net Communications, put the issue of shared agenda most succinctly and clearly: "We connect over what needs to be done."

> "This bothers me, the way some people are always sizing each other up, trying to figure out what someone else can do for them. I once had a young person sit in my office and say to me, 'You should never waste your time on someone who can't help you.' And I said to him: 'Yes, but how do you know?'"
>
> —DONALD M. STEWART

Even though an agenda is a calculation of self-interest, it doesn't mean it's bad. Agendas are only bad if the focus is on personal gain at the expense of someone else, particularly someone with fewer resources, including less power. If you do this, you become a user, which I'll talk about more in Principle Six. Having a shared agenda is a good thing.

Without that feeling that there is a task to be accomplished together, or that there is a dream to be realized, then the relationship is in fact not a business one at all. And more importantly, shared agendas reveal people you might want to go further with—someone who may share your same values and maybe your dreams, too.

Shared Values

Danny Meyer's success in the restaurant business has been written about in the trade journals and mainstream press for years now. His model is based just as much on an old-fashioned spirit of hospitality—of making his customers feel cared-for and special— as it is about the quality of the food (which, however, is also sublime).

Meyer told me that in choosing employees, he uses a 51/49 rule. "We look for someone who we feel will be a one hundred percent employee and will see us as one hundred percent employers. We look at it as a transaction in which our employees are hiring us just as we are hiring them. And in that very first interview I say to people that what we look for is fifty-one percent emotional skills, forty-nine percent technical skills.

"I know the sort of emotional skills that are required to be part of our staff; they're things you know from second grade, but they're the things you really can't teach. The person has to be kind, be intelligent or at least curious to learn, must possess an excellent work ethic, be empathic, and be emotionally self-aware. And if a person comes in to talk to us and doesn't have those skills and those values, then the other forty-nine percent won't really matter because I won't want to learn any more about the person. I don't really care how good a waiter or a cook someone is if I know they don't share the values of the organization. Ultimately, they won't fit in and the relationship will fail."

> "The more important the relationship, the more important the values are."
> —WILLIAM ZANGWILL

Legendary sports agent Leigh Steinberg told me that when he decides whether or not to take on a new client, the athlete's values, more than his ability, are the determining factor.

"A player needs to be willing to serve as a role model, to give back to his community, to add something good to the world. It's the whole essence of how we've been successful.

"It's critical for me to have players whose values I believe in. It releases a level of energy and passion in me when I negotiate for them because I fervently

> "If you value being big and being successful, you're going to lose your confidence really fast, 'cause there's always somebody bigger and better than you. That is certainly not what I value, so it's easy to maintain my confidence out there in the world. What I value most is real people who have real integrity, who have real vision."
> —CRISTINA CARLINO

believe that they will go out there and do good things for the world. I also can feel confident in the fact that our job will be easier because we'll have a much lower incident of some of the foibles of young athletes: drugs, drunk driving, things like that. We try so hard to ensure that our clients' values are stronger than that. And of course, then, when I negotiate, the owners I deal with know that they're going to get a player who accepts that they have responsibilities, who understands that they need to be on time, who is not going to go out and get arrested for irresponsible personal behavior. It works for our business in every imaginable way."

Michael Goldstein, who is Chairman of Toys "R" Us, told me that when he was being interviewed to go to the company by the founder, Charles Lazarus, he was never asked a question about his abilities. Lazarus asked about his father, his mother, how he spent his free time. And when Goldstein tried to inject something about his qualifications, Lazarus told him not to bother: *"I know you have the knowledge, otherwise you wouldn't be where you are right now. I want to know about you as a person."*

> "My theory is that if you have common interests and a common goal, you have a partner. I've always had a partner. In marriage and in business. And the collaboration comes from fondness, kind of like a love affair. It has to do with tuning in on someone and getting the right frequency."
> —DAVID BROWN

And Goldstein went on to use that experience to form his own way of talking to people he's thinking of working with. "When I interview people, I really want to get into their values and find out what they're all about. It's not all about the skills; the skills you can learn about by reading a resume. That's not nearly enough. I need to know if they're going to be happy in an environment that's all about teamwork; and to work well with other people you need to know not just what the person knows, but who the person *is*."

Values are the decision tools people use to get through their daily business life as they achieve their agendas. They are the guidelines you use to decide what you will and will not do, especially in small situations where you think no one is watching.

Values Failures

Bob Gutenstein, Managing Director of Burnham Securities, Inc., for thirty years was a partner in a well-known Wall Street firm. After one of his partners died, Bob took over as CEO, and a few years later, left the firm to start over someplace else.

He was exceptionally generous in sharing his story, and his story was very much like many others I've heard. What happened is that when one partner died, new people came in. Their values weren't the same. I'm not saying they were bad or wrong, just not the same. What seemed like a manageable difference turned out not to be.

Without *ongoing*, explicit agreement about values, you lose the elasticity that lets relationships snap back after disagreements about money and methodologies. It is extremely easy to believe that once you agree on values, it's a done deal. It's not. Values are never over.

Shared Sense of Mission

I know it sounds corny; I could barely force myself to write the words. But it's true. Forget the buzzword stuff you've heard: I'm not about to get you to write a mission statement, don't worry. And I don't much care what your mission *is*—whether what you want out of your career is to rid the world of nuclear waste or to make a fast hundred mil and build a mansion in Beverly Hills— your mission is your mission and only you have to live with it. But the people you want as your closest business relationships better share it.

Missions are statements of organizational intent, usually long-term. My understanding of missions has come from my conversations with Fred Harmon, who has written some terrific books on the subject. Fred always points to the original NASA mission statement: Place a man on the moon and bring him back safely by the end of the decade. Missions are specific, and when you have one, you know what you won't do, as well as what you will. Marty Evans, National Executive Director of the Girl Scouts of the U.S.A., the largest organization for girls in the world, told me,

"I avoid people who are willing to be anything." She's right. To be successful, you must define yourself. What you don't want is to have a mission like so many corporate mission statements that have been massaged by committees and have become so general that they cover every possibility and, ultimately, mean nothing.

Nancy Evans, one of the co-founders of iVillage, said to me, "When I met Candice [Carpenter, her iVillage partner], there was something about her, her sense of mission, that was so invigorating and so appealing that, even though I'm usually shy, after we met the first time, I was emboldened and reached out. I sent her a note that said: 'I think we ought to become friends.'

"It sounds silly, but the best relationships are ones when you see some kind of light in the other person."

Although Nancy had a feeling about Candice, sensing a shared mission is not something that is always easy to spot. It takes time. It takes some investment. You probably won't be able to know whether or not you share this with another person until you have had a significant period of time working together, getting to know each other, sharing your professional and your personal goals. But with very few exceptions, unless your mission and the other person's are compatible, there's not a lot of potential to make magic.

SENSE OF HUMOR

I was surprised by how often top people said to me that what they look for in others is someone with whom they can have fun.

Fun?

Dick Cavanagh of The Conference Board, Inc., told me, "When I'm hiring, I look for someone with a sense of humor. Because if they have a good sense of humor, it means they have a sense of irony about situations. I think if they can demonstrate that kind of sensitive, self-aware humor, it means that they know how to size up people and situations and are comfortable with people."

Linda Srere, President of Y&R Advertising, who has a wicked sense of humor herself, told me that a sense of humor is required for survival. "It keeps you sane. You wake up every morning and you just have to think 'Shit happens, you'll deal with it, move forward, and forget about it by the next day.' "

> "Laughter cleanses you. You work better. You work closer. It's the best relationship builder in the world."
> —STEVE SIEGEL

"A guy I work with calls it the 'wheel of whim.' I mean, think of what we do for a living: We go and present a campaign, they love it, they tell us we're the best and that we're going to get even more of their business. *Spin the wheel around*. Next day we get a call: They're not approving it, they've had second thoughts. They want to see something else. *Spin it around*. Now they say we don't know what we're doing, they think we should restructure the teams. Maybe we don't get their business after all. They'd like to call a meeting with our president. *Spin it around*. We're on review. Can we come in for a meeting because they're thinking of calling in a new agency because we have no real understanding of their product. *Spin it around*. The head of marketing at the client firm gets fired, they want the original campaign back, can we produce it in two weeks? *Spin it around again*. The campaign is on the air. It really is the wheel of whim. You've got to laugh. I think that successful people do not allow the darkness, the anger, the bitterness, the disappointment, to creep in. They channel the light—and find the humor."

Nancy Evans put it a different way: "I look for people who take what they do very seriously, but don't take themselves too seriously."

And Marcia Kilgore said, "There are some people around here who I really treasure for the simple fact that I can crack up with them. When everyone has so much pressure to get their jobs done, or everyone's taking everything so seriously, it's a release. I mean, we're very serious about our work: It's our job, and, yes, we want to be as professional as possible, and we have goals and objectives to meet. But, at the same time, come on. You have to keep it all in perspective. Every so often we have to just say to ourselves, or out loud, 'Come on, it's just lipstick.' "

A TRUST FUND

There are certain tangible, concrete things that successful people use as tools in making good choices about people. And foremost among these is past experience.

Hugh Price of National Urban League, Inc., told me: "It's like football. You're working with a team, and you try to identify who's marching down the field to the end zone. You have to recognize that there are some people who like to stay in the huddle all the time, and there are some who run to the sidelines, and there are some who seem to deliberately drop the ball. There might even be one who runs in the wrong direction.

> "The superior technology is understanding how to get maximum value out of who you connect with. Because nothing is as fast as human judgment. So I can save huge amounts of time if I trust your judgment."
> —SUZANNE JAFFE

"It's a real test I use when thinking about who I worked with before and who I want to work with again. It's based on relationship and on performance: Who are those people about whom I can be completely confident that, when I really need them, they will be heading for the end zone?"

> "Unlike when you invest in stocks, when you invest in people, past performance is a pretty accurate indicator of future results."
> —WILLIAM ALDINGER

Jeff Maurer, President and COO of U.S. Trust, thinks that building strong relationships "just takes time. There's no magic formula. It takes time, and it takes a crisis or two. You can know people pretty well when things are going swimmingly: But in the face of adversity, people sometimes change. When things get tough, that's when you can really tell what people are made of and how they'll come through for you."

Neil Livingstone, Co-chairman and CEO of GlobalOptions LLC, called it "having their measure." "Having someone's measure means knowing them long enough that you know their business ethics, know their reliability, know if they're trustworthy or not. In our business—and I think in almost any business these days—you need to be able to predict how someone will perform because you really don't get too many chances to do the job right."

Business is an arena in which all the agendas are not on the surface, in which many people can profit in many different ways, in which alliances and even relationships can be used and bartered and undermined in search of profit.

The most important thing to know, when picking a person to sit on your board, is: Does he deserve your trust? Can you be certain that he will not deceive you, that he does not have an agenda that is being kept secret from you?

Trust is a difficult and elusive quality. It is so rare and so important, yet so easily broken. Some people are so tentative about granting their trust to others that they remain stuck in the terrible place of trusting no one.

Without trust, you listen defensively, you look for what's hidden, you are suspicious of what might be missing. Without trust, you don't feel free to share all your ideas, all your vulnerabilities.

But when you feel trust for a particular person, it could not be clearer. You know that this is a person with whom you can be yourself, share your goals, talk about difficult issues, and brainstorm solutions. When you trust someone, you know that you don't have to hold back, and you don't have to worry. You can work together without reserve to get the job done.

Many of the people I talked to for this book told me that they depended on their instincts about whom to trust and did so almost immediately upon meeting someone new. Others told me that they felt trust was earned, and that they never trusted anyone until they had been through long periods of working together. Still others said that trust only came through shared adversity. When a crisis or two had come and gone and a colleague held on to her trust throughout—then it was hers for good.

Barbara Corcoran says that, as far as trust is concerned, "I have an instinctive gut reaction the minute I meet someone. Either I feel I can trust them and I go with it, or it's not there, period."

Cathie Black, President of Hearst Magazines, is one of the most powerful executives in magazine publishing. The entire stable of Hearst Magazines falls under her direction, including *Cosmopolitan*, *Esquire*, *Redbook*, *Good Housekeeping*, and a Hearst joint venture with Disney's Miramax, Tina Brown's *Talk* magazine. Cathie had a very different opinion on feeling trust: "It's a little bit of pick and shovel work. I have to be very careful of the big mouths—there are so many gossips in our industry, people who give quotes to the press and build their profiles that way—and those are people who you cannot trust. There are always people who will answer the exact questions you put to them, but hold back the rest of the story that they know you need for a complete picture. Those people may think they deserve your trust: They haven't lied to you. But, of course, it's just as bad. Everybody's got an agenda—and you have to be very careful about who you trust. And choose wisely. The higher up you are in an organization, the more careful you need to be."

Julie Daum, who is the Managing Director of the U.S. Board Services for Spencer Stuart, one of the most powerful recruiting firms in the nation, specializes in placing candidates on corporate boards of directors. Her method of gaining a feeling of trust in someone she meets is a combination of gut and research:

> "Look, if you don't trust, that means you can't delegate. You can't delegate, you can't run a business. Very simple."
> —EDGAR M. BRONFMAN, SR.

"I must admit, I think some of it is an intuitive feel. It's hard to get around that. I meet a lot of people through interviews, and I get to ask questions; I try to ask questions that people don't expect, so I can get an untrained response. I always throw into the conversation, somewhere where it really doesn't belong, 'How would your wife or husband describe you?' I often get a very unusual response; and that's okay. It means that at that moment I'm getting to see the real person. And I know that if the person I'm talking to doesn't let their hair down a bit at that question, then maybe they are too guarded to really be open."

Harold Evans, who has held numerous executive positions in publishing, most recently as Vice Chairman and Editorial Director of the New York *Daily News*, *Atlantic Monthly*, and *U.S. News and World Report*, said, "If somebody I really value and trust recommends a third person to me, that person has a tip to the scale that others don't. But ultimately it's about reliability over time."

The quickest way to cultivate trust is also the scariest: It's when you dare to tell someone the truth, even when doing so puts your own short-term interests in jeopardy.

Remember when, in *Miracle on 34th Street*, Santa Claus sent Macy's clients to Gimbel's? It was the perfect relationship builder because it meant that Santa cared more about the kids than the next transaction. Kids and their moms trusted this Santa more than Santas who were steadfastly flacking their bosses' product.

It works in everything else, too, as I keep learning over and over in my life. My most important client is a woman we will call Christy. We've worked together for years now and were feeling particularly close a few weeks ago. She told me that what she valued most were the times I had told her things that she didn't want to hear . . . and she knew that I was willing to risk her ire, and our future business dealings, to make sure she knew things I thought she should know.

I remembered those times clearly and how I agonized over telling her. And I remembered how much I truly didn't want to tell her. But it is in those moments that you act outside of your immediate interest that trust is built. Not in the smarmy way of the salesperson who tries to make a deal by saying, "My manager is going to kill me for this," but in the everyday course of business.

Trust is cultivated when a customer or client or colleague feels that she is being regarded and considered as more than just prospective income.

No method for finding people to trust is an infallible one, and no one method works for everybody. The point is that you need to be able to feel confident in your own ability to trust, to be open, to feel the strength of intimacy. In a very real sense, it doesn't matter if you're right or wrong about trust. Even if you put your faith in someone who turns out to be unworthy of it, the fact that you felt it when you felt it proves something about you: about your ability to be open, to share your secrets, to communicate. Its effect on a business is enormous.

Jim Farrell told me: "You've got to have trust in an organization, or the whole system collapses. We trust our people completely: We have no systems in place to catch people or look over their shoulders. And maybe if there was someone untrustworthy, they could hide here for a year or two. But once a breach of trust is discovered, that person is history."

But as Steve Siegel told me, "Because I choose to trust, some-where in there ten people are going to disappoint me, ten people are going to take advantage of me, and ten are going to hurt me. But I'm still better for it at the end of the day."

Jim Farrell points out the practical business perspective:

"If you suffer any question about trust, then you have to add a level of auditors and controls to your business—ways to catch people doing bad things—and that's no way to do business. Lack of trust costs money, it's nonproductive and it's intimidating. It keeps you from doing things as opposed to taking chances."

BAD STOCKS?

Successful people understand that a great deal of the pleasure of success is the ability to share it with people they enjoy. There's nothing better than celebrating a business triumph with people who are enjoying it as much as you are: who can laugh freely and hug unceremoniously and bask in the pleasure that comes from shared achievement and success.

They know that the best people with whom to share their dreams are those who have a similar vision of the world: who work hard, who care, who have desire, whose values they believe in, whom they can trust.

While that should seem obvious, I've come to realize that it is in fact quite different from what people who are not successful look for in other people.

Where successful people ask themselves "*What can we do together?*" unsuccessful people ask "*What can he do for me?*"

Unsuccessful people look for *the right person*—someone who can save them. They don't have a clear view of their own personal business agenda, so they don't know how to look for someone to share it. Instead, they search in vain for someone, a rich and powerful mentor, on whose coattails they can ride to the top. They want the magic of someone who will do it for them, instead of looking for a partner they can do it with.

But of course, that never happens. Because the people with the vision and the leadership want to be surrounded by other people with the same qualities.

In the absence of people who can be really helpful, unsuccessful people tend to surround themselves instead with people who make them feel good. And what makes them feel good? People who spend their time bitching and complaining about the same things they do.

The chemistry they end up looking for is the chemistry of victimization. And while they may spend a good part of their time laughing, it's not really fun. They bond over how terrible things are at the office and it almost always leads

> "There are times where you may have a choice as to who to do business with. If one of the choices is a situation that in some ways seems more desirable, but requires dealing with a bestial, manipulative guy you don't trust, that's a factor to think about. That's where you have to float back on your values system and say, hey, life is too short. The emotional cost of dealing with this person is not worth having the transaction."
> —LEIGH STEINBERG

> "Some people are molecules in motion, hoping that they will glue themselves to another molecule. And they tend to think: 'Well, gee, if I can stick to a senior level molecule, so much the better.' And they just keep popping around out there, getting nowhere."
> —DON DUCKWORTH

to rage. They don't truly enjoy the people they're connected to; they enjoy the sharing of pain.

CHOOSING TO TRUST

One of the biggest surprises for me in the interviews was that successful people *choose* to trust, as a business strategy. Don Soderquist, Senior Vice Chairman and COO of Wal-Mart, offered one of the clearest explanations of choosing to trust. He also pointed out that trusting is not the same thing as leaving cash drawers open.

"The world of retailing historically has been the buyer on the side of the retailer and the salesman or marketing person on the side of the supplier. We have learned to begin by building a trust relationship between the senior executives in both organizations— and we say, 'Hey, let's work together at all levels in our organization to do everything we can for the customer.' Now we need to try to figure out a way that we can work together to be the most effective and efficient we can, so that we can provide the lowest price for our joint customer. And what it takes is building trust.

"We have given all of our suppliers who choose to access into our computer directly over the phone lines. From a terminal in their office they can extract data from our database on all the merchandise they sell to us. In order to do that, you must trust them to not misuse that data and give it to our competitors; otherwise, we would never make that data available to them. And we're doing this free of charge."

Pat Zenner told the same type of story about one of his company's first major joint mergers.

"Over the years, Roche basically wrote the book on successful co-marketing ventures in the pharmaceutical industry," he said. "One of the things we learned early on is how important it is that there be good chemistry, trust, and shared values between the parties involved. If the chemistry isn't good, and the values between the partners aren't aligned, then you're going to run into problems because it's the natural tendency of competitors to be competitive. So, no matter how good the product is, you're going to wind up spending a lot of time trying to sort out your business relationship rather than focusing on beating the competition.

"In our situation, we developed a philosophy that simply said, let's go and beat the hell out of the competition. Once we agreed on that objective, we were able to overcome internal issues throughout the organization. With that fundamental philosophy driving us, we worked hard to solve any problems that got in the way of our overall goal. We wrote a contract, but it was put in the drawer, and we never looked at it again because it was our agreement and alignment as business partners that guided us.

"Too frequently, when you go into a business relationship or a negotiation, it's a situation where each party is trying to see who can get the last trump card. In my business experience, those kinds of relationships are never successful. The successful ones occur where there's give and take and trust; where the partners try to do the best thing together, as opposed to getting the best thing out of one another."

And in an incredibly powerful interview, Martin Yudkovitz took me through stories on NBC's joint ventures with organizations including Microsoft and iVillage, which couldn't have happened unless, at a certain point, two people had decided to trust each other.

"You have to be able to say 'we're here in the room talking about the MSNBC news service.' And while the other things will impact those discussions, we know that on that we're partners. Flat out. We're married. And on the other things, we're going to have to deal with it. And it's always going to be complicated, and it's never going to be clean."

Martin also reminded me that even for joint companies like this, trust is personal, not organizational.

BEYOND PICKING STARS

This chapter has been about how you know the right kind of person for your board when you run across one. Now let's take a look at how to make sure you're considering a broad enough spectrum of possibilities.

Diversify Your Holdings

"I always look for the opposites in everything, and that's who I pick. I think 'What do I lack?' and that's what I look for; I do it in marriages, I do it in business relationships, I do it in friendships. There's nobody like me among the people I spend time with."

—BARBARA CORCORAN

THERE'S A LOT OF TALK ABOUT DIVERSITY IN AMERICAN BUSINESS. LIKE other perfectly good words that become politically correct, it's sometimes hard to know what people are actually talking about when they talk about diversity.

So I want to make sure that I am absolutely clear about what I mean when I advocate diversifying your holdings. For me, diversifying your holdings is an investment strategy. Pure and simple. This is not a "pink" principle about how we should all feel good about one another, hold hands, and sing "Kumbaya" despite the fact that we come to the workplace with wildly different backgrounds. This is a "blue" principle, in fact, a navy blue principle, which is about how to improve returns from your people portfolio.

Let's go back to the world of financial investments. Do you have any mutual funds? I bet you do. And I bet that one of the reasons you bought them is that someone you talked with or something you read convinced you that diversification is a good way to get better returns, with less risk.

What is diversification? Simply not putting all your eggs in any one basket. You don't want only stocks. You don't want only bonds. You don't want only gold. Or vintage Barbie dolls. You want different kinds of assets that tend to rise and fall in opposite cycles, so one's up when the other is down. The idea is that some of your assets should always give you growth. And some of them should always protect you against risk.

> "With the increased diversity of workers, people are coming with different background values, objectives, and goals. I think people want their differences accommodated, and that the successful enterprise, I believe, is going to figure out how to have internal relationships that value differences."
>
> —CYNTHIA METZLER

More growth. Less risk. Sounds great, right? (The only time it doesn't feel great is when someone else puts everything they've got on one play and it pays off big-time.)

Now let's go back to Me, Inc. You want Me, Inc., to grow. You don't want Me, Inc., to fail. You want people who can help you increase your value. You also want people who will protect you from doing things that could destroy value. That's why you need a diversified people portfolio.

DIVERSIFYING FOR GROWTH

"Growth" choices are people who can tell or show you things you need to know to improve your performance. Remember, in diversifying, you want to balance the strengths and weaknesses Me, Inc., already has—your own.

Are you a marketing person who breaks out in a sweat when you have to calculate a percentage without a calculator? You may want to invest in at least one person who plays number games in her head for fun. Do you spend so much time at your computer that you order pizza on-line from the deli downstairs because it wouldn't occur to you to actually get up and go there? You may want to invest in someone who goes out of his way to talk to everyone and who belongs to everything.

Alberto Vitale, former Chairman and CEO of Random House, told me, "Early on in my career I would go to parties of my warehouse man, for instance. I was very lucky as I would go with my wife, who is very gregarious and easy to be with. And there we would be with these people, on the floor of the warehouse, one-on-one, without any distinction of demeanor or attitude, and we were one of them. That's the point: You have to be one of them. Whoever it is you're with, you have to be one of them. Then if you are, you become part of the 'community.' These days everyone's talking about community, the Internet, and becoming part of a community of people. So if you are with warehouse people, you talk warehouse, or you talk kids and family. Or if you're with IT people, you talk computers, and you talk kids and family. If you are with editors, you talk books, and books, and books, maybe family and kids, but less so . . . If you're with marketing you talk about customers, you talk about how smart the editors are. If you do that, you identify yourself with the constituency you are dealing with, and you can get a lot of mileage out of it because they talk to you openly, freely, they give you information, they give you advice. You don't have to take it, but often it's good advice, and it's there for free."

Growth choices also include those people who are just plain better at doing something than you are, including what you do for a living.

This is one of the places a blue style comes in handy. Bonding over skills and tasks is the best way to invest in someone who is otherwise your opposite.

> "A big part of good leadership is the ability to listen to other people who come at a problem in a different way. I insist that in my circle there be people with different backgrounds, different points of view, different experiences. Because the possible solutions that you come up with are so much richer from having people who start from different places. I mean, one person knowing all the answers is terrible and boring; twenty-five knowing the same answer is no better. The reason to have the other twenty-four people around is to get some new, different, exciting answers."
>
> —SHELLY LAZARUS

Years ago, when I worked for the chairman of Prudential, he asked me to organize the content for a special meeting of the company's board. The groundwork was going to be directed by Michael Russell, who worked in the London office. I had never met anyone quite like Michael and wasn't sure what to think at first.

Michael comes from a very old and distinguished family and looks and speaks exactly as he ought. Colored shirts with wide stripes. A tightly rolled umbrella. The ability to suggest, with no irony, that we might want to try the gulls' eggs at the Savoy. Our first lunch together was in the City tradition, which meant that it lasted forever, and I had to eat roast beef and Yorkshire pudding in the middle of the day and then stay awake for afternoon meetings after doing so. A significant challenge, even without the port.

Although we've never discussed it, I know that both of us went into that experience wondering if we would ever be able to understand a word the other said, let alone work together. We had a different perspective on every issue, which meant that every decision we made was better. The meeting went spectacularly well.

I learned a tremendous amount from Michael, including that crème brulee is supposed to be cracked at the table with a tiny silver hammer made specifically for that purpose, that different guild halls work best for different events, and that the smartest way to have the caterer charge for liquor was not the one I'd always used. I also learned that the best working relationships can be with those entirely unlike you.

DIVERSIFYING TO REDUCE RISK

Think about it. Are your closest business associates people who are just like you? Are they people who come from similar backgrounds? Do you find that you agree with them pretty much about everything? If so, Me, Inc., is exposed to too much risk.

It's very safe and warm to be in a group that's "just us." It's easy to focus on the things that you share and not the things that separate you. Like a group of expatriates living in Paris, you can rely on the external things you have in common to serve as your bond.

And if you think that kind of safe-and-warm choosing of people is going to work for your long-term career goals, *think again*.

Donald M. Stewart was a rising young executive in the 1960s and early '70s, when young African American men were rare in executive suites and at the higher levels of academic institutions.

He said to me: "It's very hard. Even when we live an integrated life, socially and professionally, we sometimes feel more comfortable with people we are like racially. But you have to consciously work at the

> "The biggest risk you run in life is having fifteen people sitting around a table all agreeing with everything you say. If that's the environment you work in, you're going to blow up one day."
> —KEN LANGONE

other. It's good for life, it's good for business. It's so easy to slip and always stay with your own group, but if you do it, I don't see how you can succeed in the world."

Limiting yourself to relationships with people who are like you, who see the world in the same way you do, is one of the most dangerous things you can do in your career. It's smooth and wonderful, it feels great, it's congenial, it's collegial, it's reassuring. It's all of

> "The work that my parents did was good work, and noble work. And I think early on it was clear to me if I wanted to do this good work I would need to be surrounded by people who had access to different resources than the ones I would have."
> —HANS HAGEMAN

those things until the day you walk off the edge of a cliff that no one in your crowd even noticed was there.

The problem is that when everyone around you sees the world the same way, you collectively narrow your scope of vision. It's like looking through a telescope at a building several miles away. You might have a very clear view of that building—in fact, you might have the clearest view of anybody in town—but what about everything else that's outside your narrow focal point? What about the trees? The bridges? The other buildings? You'll miss them because you have no peripheral vision.

> "Often you find yourself hiring people you like, who have a style like yours. . . . Then you find that you agree with them too much. It's very dangerous to always agree with someone. Together, you can make some really big mistakes."
>
> —WILLIAM MORIN

People who are like you see the same opportunities that you see, and they handle problems the same way that you do. People who are not like you bring new opportunities, new ways to solve problems, new perspectives on handling relationships and creating new business. The very fact of their differentness is what makes them valuable to you.

Look outside your own area of familiar comfort when you bring people into your inner circle and build a personal board of directors. Look for people of the opposite sex, other races, other class backgrounds, people with different cultural identities and political affiliations, styles, attitudes, and even, to a limited extent, values.

FIVE TIPS ON DIVERSIFYING

Invest in a high risk "stock." Look, it may well be that new person who needs a hand will never be in a position to be helpful to you in any way. There is no guarantee that if you spend time with someone who has nothing going for him but a dream, you will feel glad you did it later. His dreams may not come true. Or, as soon as his dreams come true, he may dump you quicker than an aging Hollywood actor loses his first wife. It happens.

On the other hand, the strange-looking soul from down the hall could have a great idea for the project that you can't crack.

Invest in another sector. A common career trap is spending all your time with people who do exactly the same thing you do, right now. That works really well until the time comes that you want or need to do something else.

Find a few people who are really good at a skill you "minor" in. It may be that you are working as an attorney, but that you love dance. Combine your volunteer

> "With my business partner, Esther Kaplan, we trust each other in a deep way. I don't ever agree with her, she never agrees with me, but we respect each other. That's what I think it is. We respect each other. We acknowledge the opposite's strength. So she breathes in, I breathe out, she breathes in, I breathe out. That's pretty much . . . we don't reverse it, I don't breathe in, and she doesn't breathe out."
> —BARBARA CORCORAN

work with the desire to get closer to people who know about dance. You'll learn more and have more options when the day comes that you decide one more acquisition, and you'll turn into a pumpkin.

Invest internationally. One of the best ways to understand the limits of your own cultural perspective is to see a problem through the eyes of someone from another culture. That's why travel is so wonderful, of course.

But it's also one of the wonderful things about the workplace, where you can have people from very different backgrounds all working toward the same goal—but from their own perspectives and biases. Aggressively seek out those who come at things from a different background than yours. These are invaluable relationships, tremendously educational, and worth significant investment.

Invest in different maturities. At any point in your life, it's easy to fall into an age ghetto. All your work buddies are young people who like to have a beer after work, or everyone you know has had enough of the daily grind and spends a lot of time calculating whether or not their pension will afford them a lifestyle that doesn't involve involuntary simplicity.

Force yourself out of your age range. When you are just entering the labor force, invest in one or two people whom you suspect are talking about retirement. The payoffs are that you have someone to ask about cultural references you'd be clueless about otherwise. A classic example of this kind of investing is mentoring.

Ira Millstein, a well-known antitrust litigator who is a Senior Partner at Weil, Gotshal & Manges, told me a wonderful story that illustrates the value of diversity over time. His senior officer, Frank Weil, championed his education as a lawyer. "He took my wife and me in hand and taught us about dinners and meeting clients and how to hold a knife and fork and so on."

Because Ira Millstein had Frank in his life, he had an advocate and companion who could help him navigate what Ira calls "the rest of it"—the non-legal skills it takes to build a great law firm.

The people you invest in may not be able to give you back anything today, other then their respect and energy. Someday, though, when they're in their prime and you're not, a decision to help someone on an entry-level rung could turn out to have a phenomenal payoff. If you're a young buck, remember there's a reason why that veteran lost half an antler. Knowing how it happened could save yours.

Invest in other asset classes. You have some idea about yourself and where you stand in the organization. It's sort of like high school. You are cool and have a future. Or you are worried that you aren't cool and so just buckle down and work twice as hard. In the informal part of every organization, there are similar categories, and you have some sense of where you fit. In the formal part, there are categories as well. You are the secretary, and they are bosses. You are the temp, and they are employees. You are the CEO and they are not.

Alberto Vitale said: "One of the things that I have always done during my career is to spend a lot of time with young people—or just people, not necessarily young—but 3, 4, 5, levels down into the organization. I learned this from my earlier experience working in a typewriter plant. I'd never worked in a plant before, but I discovered that the state of Connecticut had a free machinists' course. So, I took the course and became a licensed machinist in the state of Connecticut. It was very interesting because I got to know not only the people who were doing piecework, but I also met a lot of the supervisors. When I finished my course, and I went back to what I was doing—production control, finance, personnel, IT, that type of thing—I began to go to the supervisors on the floor who didn't report to me because they were the ones who used the information; they were the recipients of the services of management. They would say, "Those morons upstairs, you know, they wouldn't listen to me. We told them to do this and that six months ago, a year ago, and they wouldn't do it, but if they had done it we wouldn't have this problem." And without batting an eye, I would go back to my office and do exactly what they said, and it *worked all the time*.

Invest in categories that are not in your asset class to provide yourself balance and opportunity for growth. Been there forever and become kind of a "bond"—reliable, productive over time, no surprises? Find someone who is brand new, maybe a little rough around the edges, but also may be capable of creating tremendous value. Know deep down that you are some kind of hot stuff? Find a secretary who's been around long enough to see other stars burn out.

PUTTING DIVERSIFICATION INTO PERSPECTIVE

No investment strategy is right for every occasion, and diversification is no exception. Here are the times to think twice before you act.

1. *When you don't know your own value.* The idea of diversifying is based on rounding out the holdings of Me, Inc. That requires, though, that you have a pretty strong sense of the value of Me,

Inc. If you don't know something about what you are and what you bring to the market, diversifying is going to be tough. We'll talk more about that in Principle Nine.

The biggest issue here is insecurity, which can have a lot of causes. You may be justifiably insecure because you don't know as much about the task you're supposed to be performing as you would like to know. Time will cure that. Once it does, you can diversify.

Another issue is just plain lack of confidence. That kind of insecurity is crippling and kills a lot of deals. If you know you are insecure, work on that first, however it makes sense for you to do so—physical challenges, a spiritual practice, or counseling. Otherwise you won't be able to attract and hold the very people who would be the most valuable to you.

Sometimes it's hard to know your own value because you believe that you are "other," and that, as such, your value is discounted. You may be "other" because of how you see yourself or how the world sees you. Having experienced myself as other, I know how hard it is to reach out when it feels all you can do is hold on for dear life.

The interviewing process clarified my thinking about "other," though, and a story Don Stewart told reminded me that one of the best cures for being "other" is to concentrate on how you can contribute to performance.

Don's story took place a long time ago. He said, "It's not easy being the other. I remember when we were very new to Atlanta, we were invited to someone's home for an afternoon where there were several children the same age as my son. The other kids all knew each other, and my son was clearly the outsider; we were perfect strangers and the only African American people there. There was a beautiful swimming pool in the backyard, and all the kids were in the pool playing water polo or something like that— and they were just ignoring my son, as kids will often do around someone new.

"I could tell that my son really wanted to play, but didn't know how to go about it. I didn't think I should do anything to make the introductions—it was something he had to face. So he just got into the pool.

"My son began slowly inching himself up closer and closer to where the kids were playing; and his body language began participating: following the path of the ball, moving as the other kids moved. He kept just easing his way closer into it until, finally, the ball got out of some kid's hands and came his way. He caught it and worked himself into the game, and, within an hour, he was part of the gang." Including yourself in the game is the beginning of helping the rest of the team win.

Besides, all the time you're thinking you're the "other," they're probably thinking the same thing.

One of the biggest surprises for me in doing the interviews was how many of my interviewees saw themselves as the "other."

This is not a place for me to attribute quotes, but in virtually every interview there would be an aside, like, "Well, I was an Italian and the Irish guys were running the show," or, "I didn't go to an Ivy League school and everyone else there not only had, but belonged to the right clubs," or even, "They thought I was really pretty, so they didn't take me seriously."

After the first dozen or so of these, I went on a hunt for someone who didn't think she was the "other." Was there anyone out there who absolutely, totally, had confidence that she belonged? There must be someone out there, but I didn't run across her.

This finding came as a big relief to me since, as you may have already long since guessed, I am a graduate in good standing from the Woody Allen School of Self-Esteem.

The point is that it's easy to think you're worthless when you're

> "Having the experience of being an 'other' of some kind is life-shaping. You have to learn to get through it knowing that you are achieving against standards you value. The alternative is to let it break you. If you make it through, you have a greater confidence in yourself than do others who haven't been tested in this way."
>
> —JEAN HAMILTON

> "I can remember sitting at a table with a group of associates talking about diversity, as part of our diversity program. And a woman sort of attacked me, saying, 'Well, you just don't understand. You just don't know what this is all about. You're just—look at you' because I was president of the company. I said, 'Hold on a minute. Growing up, I couldn't speak English, my parents had no money, and I didn't know where our next meal was coming from. Don't put me in a box because of how I appear.' It's interesting how people categorize. But you can't do that."
> —CHRISTINA GOLD

the poached sole on a steakhouse menu. Easy, but wrong.

2. *When your task requires total focus on just a few people.* There are going to be times in your career where you are on the equivalent of a SWAT team and just a few of you have to get something done. It is an exhilarating time and my experiences on teams like that have been wonderful. It's particularly great during the times business feels like battle and everyone's focus is on a single, tight objective. Those times can go on like love affairs, usually between six and eighteen months. Enjoy them. As hard as they are and as much as you'll complain, you'll look back on them fondly.

But if you are still caught in that tiny web of people after eighteen months, step back and reconsider. It is probably time to refocus on diversity. Redouble your efforts to reach out. It will be harder because you will have let many of your relationships slide. Letting go for more than eighteen months will only make it more difficult.

As one investment banker said to me, "Friends just have to understand when you can't talk to them for a couple of years." Real friends will. Business relationships may not.

3. *When you lack the commitment and skill to manage a diversified portfolio.* Every time you add an investment, you have to know something about it. Every time you buy a stock, or a mutual fund, or anything, don't you spend some time learning and keeping up with it? The same thing goes for adding new kinds of investments

to your portfolio. They take more time, especially if they are some-how new to you. There is more opportunity for misunderstanding, more need for communication. Just plain more work. Don't diver-sify just for the sake of having done it unless you are willing to put the time and effort into understanding the other person and what makes them tick.

The other time not to diversify is if you have problems accepting feedback. Most of us can hear things from some people that we can't accept from others. The more unlike you a person is, the harder it can be to hear his feed-back. Maybe it's because differ-ences can keep us from feeling connected to one another. Or because different cultures have different ways of handling disa-greements.

To manage diversification ef-fectively, you have to be in the flow, considering new possibili-ties. Because the universe of pos-sibilities is literally limitless, that might seem a little daunting. The good news is that with a more specific idea of what you are look-ing for—the compliments and contrasts to Me, Inc.—it's a job that can be done. It's also a job that gets easier over time because the people you have reached out to who aren't like you will naturally take you to others you wouldn't have encountered any other way.

The hard part is forcing your-

> "One time I had a CEO invite me to serve on his board. I asked him a question: 'I've heard from time to time that you've tried to fashion your company in the eyes of investors as being another Home Depot. Does the fact that I'm one of the founders of Home Depot have anything to do with the fact that you're inviting me onto your board?' He said 'Yes': I appreciated his honesty. 'Okay,' I said, 'Let me ask you a second question: Are you comfortable having me on your board knowing that if I thought you were doing a poor job, I would be prepared to propose that you be terminated? Don't answer that question. I'd like you to think about it and call me back if you still want me to serve.' I never heard from him again."
>
> —KEN LANGONE

self to take the first step. It's like going to the gym for the first time. You're not exactly racing out the door to get there. And you can barely move the next day. But with time, this changes. You do find yourself dashing off at lunchtime to squeeze in a workout because you feel better when you exercise and you eventually love that feeling, or at least are capable of remembering in advance that you're always glad you did it after it's over.

PRINCIPLE 6

Don't Waste Time on the Wrong People

"Nobody is perfect about spotting users and people whose values aren't what they should be. Think about Jesus Christ. Jesus had twelve disciples and, of those twelve, three presented problems. Thomas doubted Him, Peter denied Him, and Judas betrayed Him. One would assume that He should be a superb personnel director. If He could have twenty-five percent of his team be a disappointment, then I know for sure that my track record isn't going to be one hundred percent either."

—Don Keough

A few years ago I met a terrific woman writer, let's call her Shirley Gooch, at a party given by a mutual friend who thought I would like to meet her. And she was right. I enjoyed several of Shirley's books, respected her work, and was thrilled at the opportunity to see her in the flesh instead of just in print.

At the time, I was still working on Wall Street, and starstruck by the idea of someone who made a living as a writer. Within moments of our talking at that dinner table, I was disarmed. She was charming and funny and smart and thoughtful. We were able to talk seriously and laugh wildly.

It turned out that she was in the middle of writing her newest book when we met; and it turned out that the subject matter of the book was the power brokers on Wall Street—a subject with which I was intimately familiar, having worked there for many years. So, I did what I could to help her with the book. I got my company to give her access to people and research, I introduced her to some other people she interviewed for the book, and I helped her think through some of the issues.

I gave a lot to this woman because I admired her and I believed in what she was doing. We had a good time together and for me as a marketing person in financial services, it was glamorous and sexy. And it had business potential: She talked a lot about how we could work together on other projects, how she could speak at company conferences and things like that. Of course, part of it was that I wanted her to admire me as much as I admired her. After the research for her book was finished, I got a gushy note from her that thanked me for all that I'd done for her, said that I'd become like a sister to her, and asked the rhetorical question: How did she ever get along without having me in her life?

I was profoundly touched by what seemed to be her utter acceptance of me and the start of our personal relationship. I treasured the note.

A few weeks later, I called Shirley to invite her to a charity luncheon I was hosting, and the response that I got from her was openly dismissive. She made it clear that she no longer had any time for me and was on to other things.

That phone call threw me. I went home and beat myself up over being so stupid as to believe that someone as successful as Shirley could have ever really wanted an honest and mutually engaged relationship with me.

Later, I heard from other people that Shirley was just a garden-variety user—and users are one sort of person that successful people weed out. One of the things that came through loud and clear in my talks with successful people is that they do not waste time with the wrong people.

In the same way that they have very clear criteria on whom they want in their circles, they have very clear opinions on the sorts of people they want nothing to do with. Bad relationships drain energy, they drain power, they hurt effectiveness. They also take inordinate amounts of time—which is one thing that successful people know they absolutely cannot afford to squander. Successful people, whether they do it consciously or by instinct, are good at separating themselves from the people who would drag them down—and that ability helps them to soar unencumbered.

They look for patterns of behavior or for personality traits that are inconsistent with what they believe are the requirements for success, and when they find them, they limit their exposure.

I'm sure that, like me, you've had someone worse than a Shirley Gooch in your life—someone in whom you've invested time, energy, and emotions, and the return on your investment has been worse than a big goose egg, it's been profoundly negative. We've spent a lot of time looking and talking about the people you should be seeking out and cultivating relationships with, but in this chapter we're going to look at the people you should be avoiding. It's unfortunate that we have to do this, but there are some people who have neither good intentions nor goodwill, and these people can be detrimental to your career if you don't watch out. Fortunately, there are only a few varieties of these people, making them easy to spot.

PEOPLE WITH BAD RELATIONSHIP VALUES

Bill Aldinger told me a story about going to visit an executive who worked for him in a site that he hadn't been to before. "This guy had been at the business for ten years. And you know what comment kept coming up about the two of us? People were asking, 'Which one is Bill Aldinger?'

"This guy had been there for ten years, and his people didn't know what he looked like! That tells you all you need to know about someone." The executive was not valuing his people's contribution to the company.

Over and over, the people I interviewed talked about avoiding people who disrespect those less powerful than they. Tom Neff, who is Chairman of Spencer Stuart, US, the country's most influential recruiting firm of CEOs and board members, said to me, "If someone calls up here and beats up on my secretary, I don't want anything to do with him. That's not the kind of person I want to deal with. I don't care how good their track record may be. If that's the kind of person they are, well, life's too short to have to deal with them, not to mention that my secretary is too important to me and the organization for me to allow her to be abused. What would that say about the values of this company?"

For Tom Neff to refuse to do business with a top corporate executive, which is the way he makes his money, is a major statement. He is saying that his secretary and the value she brings to the organization are more important than any one client or candidate, no matter how major.

Ken Langone is President and CEO of Invemed Associates, a Manhattan investment bank he founded in 1974. He is also the co-founder and Director of Home Depot, and was on the Forbes 1999 list of America's 200 richest people. "I'm very attentive to how people treat people beneath them—it's a good indicator. For example: I once went to breakfast with a potential business associate, and this fellow was all over me, sweet as pie, because he wanted something from me. But at the same time he was rude as hell to the waiter. He doesn't do it out of some warped feeling that I'll be impressed—it's just his nature. What he doesn't realize is that I now know that he can't relate to the people who have to perform the basic tasks, the tasks that make us all look good—or if he does relate to them, he does it in a very negative way.

"In a similar fashion, I am given great pause if I see that some-one's assistant is frightened or intimidated. Because that means that people below him are being sent a signal that they can't open up, can't talk freely for fear of reprisal. And, of course, that means that the executive is never going to know what's really going on in his organization because his staff is afraid to tell him. Nobody brings him bad news because they're afraid to—so he is unaware of his problems and those problems never get addressed. That's bad business."

Successful people have a deep enough understanding of posi-tional power and its limitations to know that it is bad judgment to use it as a determination of who should and should not be treated well. A person's value to a business venture may have little to do with their positional power. And often someone with very little power can be very useful indeed. And when they see someone else who does not share that basic understanding—they run.

Energy Vampires

Successful people have loads of energy, endless enthusiasm, and relentless optimism. And that takes work. And support. Nothing drives them crazy faster than people who drain that energy; and there are few sorts of people they want out of their lives faster.

Somewhere along the way I started calling people like this "en-ergy vampires"; a phrase I picked up separately and virtually si-multaneously from both William Zangwill and Linda Srere.

Linda Srere, President of Y&R Advertising, one of the world's preeminent advertising networks, said "I've always said that the best thing about this business is the people. There are people whom you work with who are absolutely incredible. They're pas-sionate, they're hardworking, and they're what makes coming to the office an adventure every day. The flip side of this are the energy vampires. These are people who steal a piece of you. Here's a quick way to spot one: They're the ones who make your heart drop when you see their number appear on your caller ID."

An energy vampire is a person who makes you tired every time they walk in the room: They just drain the life and the enthusiasm out of every situation. They're the ones who leave voice-mail messages that go on for *hours*; whose e-mails are all marked "urgent" no matter what they're about. They're usually people who have a patent disregard for—or at best a lack of understanding of—what your priorities may be. They're massively insensitive.

They also, often, waste your time by sending endless reports of activity: what they're doing, where they've been, whom they've talked to, what steps they've taken to prove that they're valuable. But those communications are rarely about actually getting something accomplished.

The energy vampires look to document their work life so that they'll have something to point to in case something bad happens. *But wait: Look how much work I did.* When, of course, all the activity they put into the documentation is actually accelerating their decline—because not only are they wasting their own time, they're wasting everyone else's.

Liz Smith, the renowned syndicated columnist, says, "People who are needy are just too hard. I feel like I have to get away from them. Even if it's somebody amusing and smart, somebody who I might otherwise enjoy. If it's someone who constantly needs something from me—it just takes up too much of my energy."

Dealing with energy vampires is unproductive in the extreme. You're giving them transfusions: You spend your time taking care of their needs, reassuring them that they're not as useless as they fear that they are. And it never stops. As long as they continue to hemorrhage with insecurity, you can pour energy into them all day every day and it never gets better for them—and you're walking around pale and lifeless.

Users
Everyone, at some point or other in their career as a relationship investor, is going to run into a user. It's inevitable. It's painful. It's one of the real hazards of forging intense relationships at work. It's like running smack-dab into a speed trap.

Getting involved with a user is one of the most complicated and perilous events in any career. It can derail you for years, causing intense emotional pain, wasting enormous amounts of time, and possibly hurting your career in ways that will surface long after your relationship with the user has ended.

And the reason it's so destructive, and so painful, is that sometimes when you get involved with a user, it can be a very intense emotional relationship. The user really knows how to manipulate your emotions and get you to believe that you're the weak one, the one at fault, the one with a problem, not him.

Users know how to get you on the hook and reel you in; they're master fishermen. And before you know it, you've been cleaned, filleted, and served on a platter with parsley and lemon.

> "We can't be victims. We do have control. That means we have to make choices about how we spend our time and whom we spend time with."
> —MARTY EVANS

Users are narcissists: They are people who are so self-directed, so self-involved, so consumed with their own needs and objectives that there's no room inside them to ever really deeply understand that people they get involved with have needs and objectives, too. Or, if they do understand it, it just doesn't seem to them like something they need to bother with—after all, their own needs are *so* much more pressing.

Users are almost always incredibly charming and attractive: It's part of the skill. They know how to use their personal magnetism to their own advantage, and they know how to keep giving you just enough light from their inner beacon to keep you dazzled and keep you from seeing just how little you're really getting from them.

They are like little nuclear reactors, energy radiating from an intense core, lighting up everything around them, but they drain power from all other sources.

I once knew a fellow who was a classic user. Let's call him Don. He was a features editor at a major glossy magazine, and he was quite enamored with the trajectory of his own career—which, in fact, had been quite extraordinary. He'd started as a kid right out

> "Just one enemy can be very expensive. If someone happens to be on a board where you're doing an important assignment and that person says to other board members, 'I'd never use that firm again, or that individual again.' Or, if somebody leaks some information or inadvertently mentions the name on an airplane, or speaks to the press when they shouldn't have, all those kinds of things can blow, not only a meaningful relationship, but multiple relationships."
> —TOM NEFF

of journalism school, typing letters for one of the editors, and within three years he had moved into a senior job himself, assigning articles, choosing subjects, working on the layout of the entire book.

He surrounded himself with a coterie of young associates who found being around him irresistible. After all, he was enormously funny, attractive, entertaining, and gossipy. And he was in a powerful position. He could have an enormous effect on the careers of any one of this group of young people he surrounded himself with—by promoting them, by assigning them stories, by easily helping them to get a job working at another magazine.

Don would always take one or more along with him to industry parties, to movie screenings, to dinner with writers who came in from out of town. These young people were swept up in the glittery trail, and were, of course, smitten.

One young woman told me: "It was an incredibly exciting time. I was just out of journalism school, and there I was, hanging out in a restaurant with Kurt Vonnegut; going to book publication parties with all the New York literati. And Don was always so much fun to be around. He treated me like I was important, right from the start."

Don loved having these young people around him: They were mirrors who reflected his glory back at him. He loved their youthful energy and excitement, their devotion to him, their endless capacity to do things he asked. By including them in his circle, he gave them a level of recognition and entrée to the world of magazine publishing that they just couldn't have any other way.

But the price was high. "Yeah, there were things about it that were great," another young man told me. "It was fun and exciting. But I just knew that Don didn't really give a damn about me. He always wanted me to go places with him, and do things for him: read a few extra manuscripts over the weekend, prepare a speech for him that it really wasn't my job to do, take care of his cats when he went on a trip. Even when I no longer worked for him, he'd call me and ask me to read something for him or to help him plan a party, all kinds of things. It was a lot of work, but it was really hard to say no to him. You know, you'd want to say no, and then he'd invite you to some gallery opening you were dying to go to, and it was so much fun to be around him, how could you say no?

"But when I finally realized that I could never get him to help me when I needed help, that he'd never return my calls when I was the one asking a favor—I had to break myself of seeing him. It was destroying my self-esteem. I could never get him to acknowledge that what I had to do was important, too. But getting away from him wasn't easy. It was like withdrawing from a drug."

Users are very good at pretending, especially to themselves. They know how to fake caring, and how to fake interest in you and your needs—and that's why you're drawn in. Nobody is naïve enough to buy into a bad user, someone who just takes and takes. Those types are easy to spot. It's the *good* users, the talented ones, that you have to watch out for. The talented user knows instinctively when to keep letting out a little more of the fishing line: when to ask after you and your career, when to focus on what you are doing, what you need. He knows when to turn down the light just enough so that you get a moment to shine.

The scary thing is that the line between a user and a person who should be on your board can be very thin. A user could well be someone who should, in all other ways, be a perfect fit for you: He could be someone who, in the best possible world, is a fantastic partner for you in your career journey.

Saying Good-Bye to a User. Getting out of a relationship with a user will not be easy. The hardest part is realizing the relationship

How to Spot a User

1. LISTEN TO OTHERS.

If you work in a close-knit business community, people will tell you who the users are; pay attention. Users are notorious for moving from one person to the next, eating up energy and spitting out the remains. If you hear a warning, pay heed.

2. LISTEN TO YOURSELF.

Pay attention to your emotions; if you have nagging instincts that someone you are involved with is a user, there's probably something to it. Ask yourself these questions:

- Do I feel good telling this person good news about myself? Do I really think he's glad to hear it?

- Do I feel nourished after I've been with this person, or do I feel depleted?

- Do I in my heart believe that this person feels as strongly toward me as I do toward him?

- Am I certain that this person would come through for me in a moment of crisis?

- Do I believe that this person would respect a confidence? Even if he could profit from passing the information on?

- Do I often feel like I've been entertained by spending time with this person, but afterward I feel empty-handed?

- Do I find myself getting obsessed with his needs, sometimes even more than my own?

- Do I routinely get mad at myself after I've talked to him because we didn't really talk about what I wanted to talk about?

- Do I really believe that when he asks me a question, he listens to the answer?

A yes answer to any of these queries could mean that the person in question is a user. Beware.

3. LISTEN TO HIM.

While a talented user is good at drawing people in, there are clues that might give him away. Does his conversation always revolve around him and his needs, and does he only turn to you and yours after it's clear you're getting annoyed? Does he say things to arouse your feelings of guilt? Like insinuating that you don't give him enough, aren't there for him when he needs you, often let him down—when you know in your soul that it's just not true? Do you feel like this person calls you when you're up and ignores you when you're down? Does this person ever talk to you about a third person—someone else who you think is a good friend to him—saying that that person is always disappointing him? Does he often say that he feels abused in relationships? That nobody understands him? Any yeses, and beware.

you have with him is not one of fair exchange. Once you understand this, you can begin to move away.

Users never see themselves as users: They see themselves as victims. They will not understand why you no longer want to spend your life taking care of their needs—all they're going to see is that you are withdrawing from them, taking away something that they need. It will feel to them like you're pulling an IV out of their arm—they will resent you.

When you stop giving a user what he wants, he will blame you: He will do everything in his very persuasive power to make you feel guilty, to make you feel bad, to make you feel like you are the one who is being selfish and self-centered. And, in his heart, he'll believe it.

And, for a while, you may lose your grip on reality. Because talented users have a way of making that happen. You will have a real emotional reaction to his pain because, in fact, his pain is real.

Do not be deterred; do not give in. If you do, it'll be even harder the next time. Remember that pleasing a user is not your life's work—even though he makes you feel like it is. Be firm. Say no. Break the pattern. Above all, get support and protect yourself.

"My experience is that the best way to respond to bullies is just a big smile, and a 'Thank you, thank you.'"
—JOHN LIMBERT

The user's personality is much like an infant's. His response will be to act out, to scream and carry on, to have a tantrum. You have to do what a parent does. Buy time. Stay calm. Distract him. "I just don't have any M&M's with me, darling. How about an apple?"

It doesn't feel good to be hated, but know this: The user will hate you when you stop playing along. You're going to have to live with that. If the user in your life is your boss, you'll have to find a new job; if it's a client, that income stream will need to be replaced.

But even when you think it's over, it's not over—because users specialize in revenge. They will feel completely justified in bad-mouthing you, in doing things to hurt your career, in taking business away from you in any way they can. They feel like you have stabbed them, and they'll want to stab you back.

And it's here where, maybe, you can do a little damage control. You'll never get them to like you, or forgive you, but perhaps you can get them to stop going out of their way to hurt you. Don't try to get them to see the truth: They simply won't. Narcissus could only see himself in the pool. Trying to get a user to see that he's being unreasonably demanding and that you were the one who was abused simply will not get you anywhere. In this one instance, if you think that a user could really hurt your career by using hardball revenge tactics, consider softball. Blame something else: or blame yourself. "This project I'm working on is taking all my time. I'm up until two A.M. every night. When it's over, let's try to get together again," or, "I know I haven't been good about staying in touch. I've just been completely snowed under." A few softballs in a row should do the job.

Of course, every once in a blue moon, you do have to play hardball. There are going to be people who mistake a desire to build trust-based relationships for weakness, and there are going to be people who are so consumed by their own needs that they don't notice yours. When I talked to Bernie Marcus about those people, he told me, "You run across people who, when they see that they're dealing with somebody who has a little compassion and emotion about humans and humanistic traits, will try to take advantage of you. Then you have to use your power. It's frightful. I hate to do it. I think in my career I've done it maybe four times. It doesn't leave you with a good feeling, but sometimes you have to do it because somebody is so bad that the only thing they understand is getting hit on the side of the head by a two-by-four. But it's not a way to conduct your life. And there are people that live their lives like this."

Remember that while sometimes necessary, hardball tactics are always the last resort. Before you make your first move, let them choose their weapons. Then you know for sure how they are going to play and are clear in your own mind about what you're doing and why. Once they prove themselves untrustworthy, you can sound your battle cry. But first, be clear that they'll hear it.

As we talked about this further, Bernie Marcus added, "I would rather build a company based on respect and love than fear and intimidation because you get a lot more."

Wouldn't you?

A DARK PAST DOES NOT SIGNAL A BRIGHT FUTURE

Successful people take chances with new people. They're risk takers, they invest in things that are unproven, hoping for a return. They look for the upside, and that often means, when dealing with people, taking a chance with someone untried or untested.

But they're not stupid. And as I've already stated in Principle Four, history matters. A lot. If you want a pretty good indicator of how people are going to behave in personal and business situations, find how they've behaved before. If you want to get a picture of how they're going to treat you, see how they've treated the people who came before you.

When I talked to Steve Siegel, Chairman and CEO of Insignia/ESG, Inc., the nation's third largest commercial real estate services company, about this, he called it personal due diligence. He told me, "I don't mean we checked somebody's background.

"**S**mart people put money into bad projects all the time with people who look good on the outside. Or if you have the old school tie, you think: 'Well, there's no need to check him. He went to Harvard, too.' "
—NEIL LIVINGSTONE

We worked to get to know one another and understand the personal aspects of whether we could work together and whether the values, the approach, the business, the relationship building, whether those components were there. It was every bit as important as the balance sheet, you know, how well did this company do and what kind of money they're making. I think for every acquisition we did, we probably passed on five because of that process.

"But you have to spend time. You learn about them. You learn about their families. If possible, during the months of financial and personal due diligence you meet their friends, you attend events with them, you meet their children, their spouses if they have them. And at the end of the day, it's your gut."

Steve Siegel went on to tell me about how this worked for him. "There was one acquisition, a pretty sizeable one that would have made a nice addition to our organization, and it was just a period of due diligence with two of the senior people. We could never break through. Never could engage in any personal dialogue. Any time the attempt was made, just in a normal course of conversation, it was instantly brought back to what's the long-term strategy? What's the capital infusion going to be? What's the ultimate take-out and earn out for us? What will we get for this and what will we get for that and what's our parachute if it doesn't work and what's the breakup? It was always right back to that. And then it repeated consistently, like drumming. At one point, I flew out to have a dinner and get close to the CEO, my counterpart at this firm. And I tried everything.

"I let him know things about my life, who I am, what I am, and when you do that, when you open yourself up to somebody who you're going to build a relationship with, they usually give that back. There was nothing. It was right back to, you know, what do we do about the national accounts? How do we roll this out? How about the overlap? What about the redundancies? How many people will we have to let go? That's all important stuff and we deal with it very effectively as our balance sheet attests to, but that wasn't what I was there for. Do I want to work with this guy every day very closely? Do I want this guy to be one of the five people in the inner circle of this organization?"

Steve Siegel didn't get involved because he realized that the only thing these people shared with his company was a common interest in this one deal. The relationship would only have been about two companies using each other. And Steve Siegel is interested in building relationships that have a deeper, more long-term perspective.

> "I've walked in places and thought, 'Oh, this is not gonna be a good meeting,' because the receptionist is not happy to see me."
>
> —BOB ANNUNZIATA

An insurance industry executive, who asked that his name not be used, told me a story about what happens when you don't do personal due diligence.

Someone had recently hired him for a job. The person apparently had a reputation for being very smart, very creative, innovative on the creative side. She had a sterling career and kept getting better and better jobs at more prestigious places. But she had never really run a big department of her own.

Then she was given the creative department of a major company to run—and she came after this industry executive to work for her. He was the number-two person somewhere else at the time; it was smaller and had less buzz than the one she was running. She was very seductive and said things like, *"It's just going to be the two of us, we'll turn the place around, we'll have so much fun, we'll shake up the industry."*

He took the job, and, according to him, it was the worst experience of his professional life. The woman had absolutely no ability to share creative control. She couldn't even really hear an idea that wasn't hers. He had ideas of his own and wouldn't give up on them. But she just didn't want to hear them. Her attitude was clear: She had hired him to serve her and to carry out her agenda without asking any questions or adding anything. Within three months, it was clear to him that this wasn't going to work out. In nine months, he was fired.

He said, "I should have known. She had never hired anybody at my level before, but people had told me that she couldn't hold on to assistants, that she was always hiring consultants once and never hiring them again. There was a pattern that very clearly indicated an inability for her to connect and stay bonded with people. She worked best as a lone ranger. But she was so damned convincing and seductive that I rationalized to myself that this time it would be different."

Could it have turned out differently? Of course it could have. Patterns are broken, people change, and sometimes if you're aware of another person's pattern, you can actively work on ways to make sure that whatever it is you don't want to happen doesn't.

But if you're not aware of someone's relationship history, or if you're in denial about it, you're in trouble. It's like investing in a company without any idea of whether or not it has ever earned a profit, or whether—at the moment you're placing your order—the stock is up or down. It's buying blind, and that's never a smart investment.

> "People I don't want to be associated with? People who have a sort of smirk, people who are cynical, people who are sleazy, people who don't respect other people, particularly those who are working for them. People whose reputation is marginal. I don't want to work with those people."
>
> —DAVID BROWN

Successful people know that before they place a big bet on someone, they must find out what their pattern has been. They ask around, they do their research. And that research is not just a resume: They know not to focus only on someone's career track and promotions. They ask what the person is like to deal with; they want to know what the other person's values are; they want to know if the other person has integrity.

Julie Daum says, "You can't just get a list of references from someone. I mean, anybody can find three or four people in the universe who like him and will say so on paper.

"You've got to talk to people. I mean, I could have a gut instinct about someone and be a hundred percent wrong. It happens. The answer is to have an informal network of people you can call— people whose values you believe in and whom you trust—and be able to say, 'So, what's the deal with this guy?' If you trust the person you're calling, and they trust the person you're calling about, you know a lot more than when you started."

That kind of gut check is one of the things you should be getting from your personal board.

And what are the negative things that successful people are on the lookout for? A lack of the personal attributes and values that are important—the things we talked about back in Principle Four. If the person in question has demonstrated a lack in those areas, keep your distance.

Do It Every Day

"One of the things I learned from Ken Roman at Ogilvy & Mather twenty years ago that stayed with me forever and that I live by to this day: He said, 'Every day you should touch an employee, touch a client, and touch a friend. Don't ever let a day go by when you haven't done that, or you will be forever playing catch-up.' "

—LINDA SRERE

BROKERS ON WALL STREET MAKE EXTREMELY NICE LIVINGS, AND THEY have done so for a long, long time. And when you stop to really think about it: What is it that they do so well? They can't all be calling the market perfectly, the research they have access to is not so hard to get in other ways—especially since the rise of trading on-line. They're not offering anything that a smart consumer hasn't been able to get a lot more cheaply for the last decade or so. Much of the actual work they do, from the outside, doesn't seem all that hard.

So how is that these people, many of whom don't have advanced degrees, do so well?

In part, they do it because they connect with their important clients in a way that makes those clients feel taken care of.

There's a huge industry on Wall Street in teaching brokers what is artfully called "contact management." Consultants are brought in, at huge sums of money, to work with the brokers and go through the brokers' "book of business," which is a list of what is often a thousand or more people with whom they do business. The lists are organized into stratum—the highest being the 20 percent of the clients who probably bring in 80 percent of the business.

These consultants then help the brokers set up software systems for keeping in touch with those core people. And the software is so elaborate, and so specific, that it can be programmed with information like, "Bill Muldoon is interested in Lucent," so that whenever something interesting happens at Lucent, a pop-up box will appear on the broker's screen that tells him exactly what happened at Lucent, reminds him to "Call Bill Muldoon," and will even, at the touch of a button, dial Muldoon's phone number.

> "The two most powerful things I know in existence: A kind word and a thoughtful gesture. And it just takes a short moment to say hi, really appreciate that note of yours, you're doing great, we appreciate all you're doing for us, stay in touch, happy holidays."
>
> —KEN LANGONE

"Good for them," you say, or you don't say if you're a competitor. Then you go on to say, "But I'm not in sales." Yes, you are. You are selling yourself and your dreams and goals as surely as brokers are selling stocks. Your success depends on connection just as theirs does, if not in the same transaction-oriented way. As I went around on my interviews, I learned that it wasn't just brokers who had a system for being in touch. Every successful person I spoke to, whether he or she was conscious of it or not, had intricate and methodic systems for maintaining relationships with people.

Successful people lead busy lives. It comes with the territory.

When you're successful, you have a demanding existence that includes being responsible for the functioning of a business and all the people that attend that business: employees, clients, investors, lawyers, consultants, media, and dozens of other sorts of relationships. Successful people almost always also have busy social lives that, in some way or other, intersect with their work lives. And they probably also have family responsibilities of one sort or another.

There are dozens if not hundreds of people who come in and out of their lives on a weekly basis—and there are probably several dozen people at least who are close enough and important enough to be candidates for a seat on their personal boards. The only way that they could possibly find the time and the energy to keep connected with all those people in a way that feels honest, intense, and real is to have systems for getting it done. They manage their time and their effort in ways that make sense, that utilize their energy effectively, but that also, always, make the other person feel important and valuable.

For some of these people, those systems are so automatic and so ingrained in their personality that they barely know that they're doing it—but they are.

I was talking to Parker Ladd, Vice President and member of the board of directors of Literacy Partners and Co-Executive Producer of *Open Book* on A&E, and I asked him if he had any systematic way of dealing with relationship issues. He looked at me like I was insane and said, "Of course not," and the conversation went on. Later I noticed that after I said something that was of interest to him, he took a note card out of a leather holder in his suit jacket and wrote himself a note.

> "**W**ork is expanding to fill all of our available time. It'll take over everything if we allow it to, but we can't become victims or let ourselves feel like victims. We do have the ultimate control, and we do have to make choices about how we spend our time. If you value a relationship, or want to enrich one that seems to need a little nurturing, you've got to *choose* to do it. The point is to make intelligent choices."
> —MARTY EVANS

I asked him how many of those cards he writes on a day. "Oh, four or five," he said. And what does he use them for? "To make notes to myself to remember to follow up on things that people tell me." Like what? "Oh, to send them a book, or to call someone else on their behalf, something like that." Oh. And is there a system for making sure that you follow through on all those notes? "Of course. I have a place on my desk where I put them every time I return, and they're the first thing I go over with my assistant each morning."

He didn't even recognize it, but he has a perfect system that not only makes sure that he remembers to follow up with people when he said he would, but makes sure that if he offers them something with value, that they get it.

People like Parker are naturals. They have a little piece of their brain that handles connection, that instinctively and intuitively knows when and how to reach out to others, and knows who in their lives needs what from them, and when. Others have elaborate methods of keeping themselves conscious and focused on the soft stuff—and they do it with the precision and timing of a computer program.

Ultimately, whether it's inborn or learned and rehearsed, successful people understand a very specific and important aspect of dealing with others that many of us pay lip service to, but that they actually *do*. And that aspect, as we discussed in Principle One, is valuing people. They genuinely feel that another person's needs are as important as their own and they have a sincere desire to satisfy those needs. It sounds easy, but it's an incredibly difficult thing to do.

It is an act of will for everyone. Many of us think, when we watch people who are good at this, that it's simply in their

> "I realized early on as an analyst that companies that were solicitous of The Street, that told the analysts a lot about what was going on, and that maintained a high level of comfort with the sell side would be recommended more often and would ultimately sell at higher P/E multiples than other, similar companies."
> —MICHAEL CULP

nature. But it's not. It's hard for everybody and it's a conscious choice that they all have to make.

They choose to engage in battle with themselves: They force themselves to face their insecurities and put other people's needs before their own need for recognition and importance. This is the thing that really separates the people who are great at relationships and the people who are not. It's the ability to go from the shining moments we all have, when we remember someone's birthday, to making it a way of living. No matter what the systems are, no matter how they remember to stay connected and what they do to heighten the connections, they strive to satisfy the other person's needs as much as their own. And it works wonders.

> "When a so-called very busy chief executive wants to do something, he can do it. And when he doesn't want to do it, he doesn't have to do it. So when you hear, 'Oh, this guy is too busy to see you or to do this or that,' it's not that he's too busy, it's just that he doesn't want to do it, for whatever reason."
> —ALBERTO VITALE

The systems that I've learned from people who do it best fall into separate and quantifiable categories of activity. These are guidelines and inspiration to help you develop and devise ways to reach out to people, build and maintain relationships—particularly among your board members—and above all, make it personal.

1. Have Reminders

We'd like to believe that the people who are important to us are on our minds all the time; but we'd also like to believe that Tinker Bell will live if we clap loud enough. When you're busy, and outside things are constantly vying for your attention and your time, it's impossible to do all the things that you'd like to do.

> "Now, you don't have to spend extra time with the bank clerk, that's not our business. In fact, you shouldn't be seeing the bank clerk. But for people who are close to you and people you rely on, that's part of the job. And it's not taking time, it's doing what you're paid to do."
> —EDGAR M. BRONFMAN, Sr.

Successful people realize that they

need reminders; that people, just like the tasks that one has to complete day-to-day, can go unnoticed and forgotten if they fall to the bottom of the pile.

So they come up with ways to remind themselves of all the people they want to keep in touch with.

Phillip Riese worked for many years in the financial services industry, many of those years at American Express, where he ultimately was president of the Consumer Card Services Group and where, in the late 1980s and early '90s, he brought together a team of people that turned around American Express's then floundering card business. He told me: "There definitely are people in business who are more highly relationship-oriented—whose very being is in the relationships they form. There are others who are more oriented in the actions of business, and the ways to make things move. I fall very heavily into the latter camp.

> "The trick is to be lazy. You just get the ball rolling: Put two people together and let them take it from there. There's nothing more exciting than helping someone find a job when you like both the person hired and the one doing the hiring. Or, when you connect an investor and a company, or set up someone for a seat on a board. You make a match, and it's a useful allocation of resources. You try to figure out which two people when put together can be more valuable than either of them alone."
> —ESTHER DYSON

"I always knew that I should spend more time developing relationships, but it's just not my natural mode. I wouldn't think about it. And, when you don't think about it, you allow people to fall by the wayside. So I made sure that I always had someone working for me who was very good at relationships. It was someone who would focus on these issues and say to me, 'You know, you haven't been out to Des Moines for a long time—you need to get out there and talk to people.' This person would go with me to all my important meetings, and then after the meeting—at which I would press the company agenda and do what I had to do to increase the business—this person would say, 'You know, that could probably have gone better. Next time you're in Chicago you need to take so-and-so out to dinner.'

"I believe absolutely that my success has been totally due to the teams that I've assembled and the people I've been fortunate enough to have work for me. In spite of that, it's just not in my nature to think about planning for relationship issues. I keep a very tight calendar that is very focused on getting things done. I just don't think of carving out the time to work on relationships—so I hire someone to do it for me. This person makes appointments and puts them on my calendar solely to help me bond with people with whom it's important to me to do so."

Remember, though, that while you can have someone else remind you to build relationships, the actual building can't be delegated. Alberto Vitale put it this way: "Relationship and authority go hand in hand. Because if you have a relationship, you also have a certain sort of authority—not in the bad sense of the word, but in the positive, constructive sense of the word. For example, if I have a relationship with you and I come to you and say, 'You know, I've thought about it, and I think we should do this, that and the other . . .' because there is a relationship, the other person will be much more likely to say 'Gee whiz, you're right,' or maybe 'You're wrong,' and the matter will be closed. If there is no relationship, there is always a hesitation, a 'let's think this through.' "

Not everyone can or needs to hire someone to help maintain relationships. Ellen Levine makes the responsibility for keeping in contact hers. She told me that she periodically takes out her personal telephone book and looks down it, page by page, to see who she feels she hasn't talked to in a while, and she calls.

"I spend a lot of telephone time," she says. "I have a husband, I have a life, I can't socialize enough to stay in touch with all the people I'd like to stay in touch with. So I make sure to use the phone and periodically call each and every person on my list just so we stay connected and keep the bonds in place." Hire someone, create a calendar, use index cards, you need to devise a system for reminding yourself to maintain your relationships.

> "Another little trick I have is I will mark out an hour on my calendar for phone calls. Every day. During that time, every day, I return business phone calls."
>
> —CAROLE BLACK

2. Make Space on Your Calendar

For too many of us, if we don't have it scheduled, we won't do it. Too many other things come along in the course of our day to distract us, to fill the gaps, to demand our attention. But if you've scheduled time to be with someone else, it's unlikely you'll cancel the meeting, even if something more pressing has reared its head. It's just too rude.

Building relationships takes time, and you need to make sure to fit those blocks of time into your schedule. For many people, recreation time is ideal for working on business relationships. Golf, lunch and dinner dates, sporting events, theater. They keep us together for long periods of time, they let the bonds grow, and they can be scheduled in advance.

David Kaiser, who is a hot Silicon Valley entrepreneur, told me, "I know that back in the eighties, the ethic was '*I never have lunch*'—I have too much money to make, too many important things to do. Now—well, my ethic is, I try to never have lunch *alone*. It's too important for me to connect with people."

> "I schedule personal meetings just like business meetings. I was a very early adopter of the Palm. It has made all my scheduling so much easier. I have my lists of who I want to see or talk with, I have all my numbers and addresses, and I have my calendar, all in one place. If I have 10 minutes, I can get a lot done, and I can keep all kinds of notes in my Palm about the people with whom I have relationships."
>
> —JEAN HAMILTON

3. Have a Great Memory, or Else Create One . . .

David Rockefeller, who is one of the wealthiest men in the world and was for eleven years the Chairman and CEO of Chase Manhattan Bank, has the most extraordinary system for handling relationships that I have ever seen.

He is now eighty-five years old, and for most of his adult life he has kept a file of index cards—there are now over 150,000 cards according to his assistant, Alessandra Gregory, who explained the system to me in great detail. Every time he meets someone new—in business, at a social event, anywhere, he goes home and writes her name on an index card, and on that card he makes notes: where he met the person, what the context was, what they talked about, who introduced them. Thereafter, every time he sees that person again, he updates her card. Where did they meet this time? Who else was there?

Mr. Rockefeller's secretary at Chase keeps this card file organized. She checks newspapers for any mention of individuals in the system and updates the cards on a daily basis. If someone has a baby, gets married, gets divorced, changes jobs, it's noted on the card.

Alessandra told me that the staff uses the cards to see exactly what the relationship is that Mr. Rockefeller has with people who call or write him. If someone calls and tells a member of the staff that "Mr. Rockefeller and I are old friends," they can see exactly how many times the two have talked, corresponded, or seen each other in the last sixty-five years.

> "I find the rudest thing is when someone doesn't return your call. And there are certain people who are terrible at that and apologize that they're just not good at it and so on. But there's no excuse. No matter how busy you are, you return the phone call."
> —MICHAEL GOLDSTEIN

Not that this is a system meant to keep people out. In fact, it's just the opposite. He does it to make sure that everyone he deals with feels that they're important to him.

When he's invited to a social event, he likes to know in advance who else has been invited, and with whom he is going to be seated. Some people misinterpret this desire, thinking that he wants to control the person with whom he's going to associate—that he might complain if he's not seated with people of the right stature. But in fact, the reason he wants to know is so he can prepare himself appropriately.

Before every social event, he reads the cards of the people he knows will be in attendance, so that he will be sure to ask about their new job, their new house, or their children. He wants to be able to say, "I haven't seen you since that dinner in Washington in 1992," and know that he's correct.

I asked Alessandra, why he does this. I mean, we're talking about David Rockefeller. He doesn't need to go to these lengths. She said to me, "That's exactly *why* he does it. He doesn't want anyone to think that because he's David Rockefeller he's too important to care about them." He knows that when you remember details about other people, it makes them feel good, and makes them feel bonded to you.

When Hans Hageman left law to found the East Harlem school, Exodus House, a private middle school for at-risk children, he was able to get initial funding with two phone calls. The right two phone calls brought him $50,000, which was enough to open the doors. He was able to make those calls because he'd learned from his parents, and their board, that if he wanted to do good work, he would need to have strong relationships with a wide range of people.

Hans also keeps his own simple variation of a Rockefeller card system—he just makes notes on business cards. He teaches his students that they need a system, too.

"I mean, I tell my students straight out—you die alone, you need to understand that. And it's who you go through the process and on the path with that—it's going to count for something. So if you are going to make anything of yourselves socially, emotionally, academically, politically, financially—you need to figure out who you're going to surround yourselves with. . . . And some of the kids are real good. They've got their own card files."

4. Make It Personal
Successful people know that to build real relationships, you need to make your contact with others as personal, as specific, as intimate, as you can. When you make it clear to someone that you've

thought about him, that you've noticed him, that you remember him—it makes all the difference in the world in building a stronger, healthier, more honest bond.

Christina Gold says, "It's not just a question of the things that you do. It's who you are and how you do them. If you just send cards or send a note or send flowers because you think that's the right thing to do, but you really don't give a damn, then it's better not to do it.

"You've got to do these things because you genuinely believe they're the right thing to do and it's natural for you. If it's unnatural for you, it won't feel genuine to the other person, and it will harm more than help the relationship. I know that there are people who send birthday cards that are clearly out of a computer system. It's insulting.

"If you get a card from your insurance agent and it feels canned, you just feel like: 'He wants me to remember him because I'm getting older, and older means closer to death.' But if he called or sent a note at some point during the year and said, 'I've been looking over your files and things look fine; please call me if I can do anything to help,' then you'd feel cared for, not just like a target for a new policy. And that makes an enormous difference in how bonded you feel toward him."

Christina Gold saw the fruits of this firsthand. When she took over the North American division of Avon, its business was in a huge slump, the cause of which is now generally agreed to have been the disenfranchisement of the company's most unique asset: the network of "Avon ladies" that have personified the business for decades.

"There was a lot of talk when I took over about how I reinstated the sending of birthday cards and things like that. The real point is that the representatives were feeling alienated from the company—they sensed from the way they were being treated by their superiors that their role in the business was no longer valued. And, indeed, we were moving away from direct selling and more toward a direct marketing, direct mail business. Costs were being cut, and the representatives were feeling that the message they were being sent was: 'Get out of the way; either do it our way or no way.'

"And we're talking about one hundred thousand people who had stood behind the company, even through several takeover attempts. At one point, they had even given up part of their own compensation to help. They had really rallied and helped save the business.

"It's not the cards, it's the genuine emotion, the type of communication, the type of people the company has managing relationships on its behalf. Those are the things that make the difference between companies that really succeed and those that don't."

Michael Goldstein gave me another example of how he reaches out: "When I was going to start again as CEO, I made a list of about fifty, sixty people who I wanted to know about before it made the newspapers, that ranged from virtually every important supplier, some investors, some security analysts, and then some other people with whom I serve on boards. I left messages. I let all of them know that something important was happening and how can I reach you in the evening or in the morning. Now, many of them were not able to speak to me for a couple of days, but they knew there was a message and that was as important as the call. One of them said my call was the first he'd gotten from top management in eighteen months . . . since I had called him saying I was retiring. And he said, 'Just tell me what you need.' "

Shelly Lazarus has a much more basic and innate system. "I'm really interested in people. I really like people, and I care about them—and I guess that because I care, I have a very good memory when it comes to people. I can remember people's names and faces, I'll remember their children's names, sometimes even after twenty years.

"I don't have to *do* anything about that, it's just the way I am. One thing I do consciously is to send a lot of handwritten notes. When I want to say something personal, I believe it should be delivered personally. I know that some people today send very personal messages, even condolence notes, by e-mail, and I just think that's hideous. It just doesn't show the proper level of respect or personal interest."

Keeping in contact with people, and doing it in a sincere and intense way, is critical for Hans Hageman since he often has to call on people for help, be it political or economic.

"The Rolodex has gotten huge over the years—but I do my best to maintain contact with people. I don't do it for any kind of immediate return. I may never need something from these people; or I may need something in five years; or I may need something tomorrow. Who knows? That's not the point. I'm not looking for something in return when I do that. Remembering them is really nice. And, sure, it lays the groundwork for other things that might come that could be beneficial down the line. But you can't do it with that in mind."

A critical component of the personalization of communication is that it be honest. You can't fake it. And, let's face it, we're a culture of fakers. We all know that there's an enormous part of our business lives in which we pretend we're something we're not, in which we try to act as if we're more accomplished than we are. People spend an enormous amount of time faking confidence in their own abilities in order to generate new business.

And, in most ways, we all feel that that's okay. Faking confidence is an accepted part of the roles we all play in business, and can in fact help you get ahead in the business community.

But faking caring will backfire every time. People smell it. If you don't genuinely care, the job will not be done as well, or you'll send flowers when they told you they hated them—but because you weren't really caring enough to listen, you missed it.

5. Know That the Medium Is the Message

For most business people, the main method of communication these days is by e-mail, a system for communication that is highly efficient, incredibly fast, simple, reliable, and, for some, deadening.

Ellen Levine said, "It's harder to form relationships these days because of e-mail. It used to be that when you talked to people on the phone, there would be the little niceties—'How are you, how are the kids,' which is of course wasted time—but kept you connected. Now, with e-mail, everyone just gets right to the point, asks a question or sends information, and there's never time for the personal. And, indeed, people are wary of adding anything personal to an e-mail message since it can be so easily forwarded to others. I think something is lost because of e-mail; it's so efficient that people no longer talk on the phone, they don't go to each other's offices or cubicles, they never get to see that there's a real person on the other end of the communication. It's unfortunate. You never get to tell a joke, to find out the other person's sense of humor, what they're like. You can't *feel* them."

But it doesn't have to be that way. Red Burns, who is one of the founders of the New York Media Association, and is widely considered one of the most influential people in new media, had a different point of view about e-mail and relationships: "I love e-mail. I love the brevity, the clarity, the one-two-three and then we move on. But I also love the fact that I can keep in touch with people who are distant, people who I'd have a hard time connecting with otherwise. It's hard with the telephone; people are busy, you play telephone tag, it takes days to connect. Or, of course, sometimes you need to communicate with someone in a distant time zone, which just makes it all that much harder. With e-mail I can stay in touch and keep myself connected day-by-day.

"I think e-mail is replacing the telephone for business communication. Telephone used to be for those things you needed a quick answer for, things that were not all that crucial. The simple, day-to-day stuff. You'd still need face-to-face for the important meetings, and that hasn't changed."

Bill Aldinger agrees: "The best thing technology has done is to get rid of a lot of the formality. You know, when I started working years ago, everybody wrote long memos and had them edited and retyped. You'd polish and polish until they looked perfect. Communication today is much better. It's a lot quicker and more personal."

Steve Siegel summed up the fact that with e-mail you need to take particular care to make an impersonal medium feel personal.

"The greatest innovation in communication is e-mail. We're an international company with fifty-odd locations and several thousand people. So now I can instantly communicate and respond to questions and deliver information anywhere. It's wonderful. And you don't lose all the time you do with telephone tag. But it takes away the personal touch. You don't get a tone of voice, you don't get inflection. You can't deliver warmth in a message when you want to send a greeting or best wishes on an important event. You can't really engage in conversation that promotes bonding. That's really it: You can't bond through e-mail."

> "E-mail is great...for people who already trust each other."
> —WICK SIMMONS

Be careful with e-mail. It's addictive and it's deceptive: It keeps you in touch with other people, but it can make you feel as if there's a bond when, in fact, there isn't. Ultimately, it's a device to convey information. It can be used as a supplement when you already have a strong relationship with someone: a way to keep in touch between other more personal forms of bonding. But don't be fooled into believing that e-mail is enough. It isn't.

My personal rule is know the person and to avoid sending bad news via e-mail—especially if the reason I want to send it that way is that I don't want to deal with their reaction.

6. Throw the Party

Part of the way successful people make connections for themselves is that they make it possible for the people they want in their circle to connect with others. In other words, they throw the party. They widen the circles. They tend to think of solutions for bringing people together in ways that are of interest to them, but they make it bigger so that it works for everyone involved.

When Raylene Decatur was stuck in a number-two job somewhere, and she was really feeling isolated and unhappy with it, she formed the "Second Banana Club"—a grouping of people in spots like hers, who could get together and talk about their shared issues: things like what jobs were opening up where, what the characteristics of a top banana were, things like that. They found things to talk about, but the real point was, they were there for one another. The club eventually broke up for the most fabulous reason I can think of: Too many of them became top bananas.

Every year Paula Gavin, who is head of the YMCA, has a gathering of people in New York who she thinks will find one another interesting. That means that every year, each of those people thinks of Paula. And when Paula calls them to serve on some committee or other, it'll be okay because she's done enough nice things and made enough connections for people that there's good will overflowing.

> "But relationships are so important, I really think that the worst mistake someone would make is not making time, because that's like saying I don't have time for myself. If you want to see someone, don't make it lunch or dinner or breakfast, because you may never do it. It will get canceled because some business thing will come up. Maybe even make an appointment if the person could come and see you in your office for half an hour, or you can see them. If you're close enough, then I think it's important to have play dates over the weekend. You must have play dates."
> —CAROLE BLACK

Edgar Bronfman told me about an annual event sponsored by his company, for a group they call the Seagram Family Association. It began as a meeting place for the sons of the Seagram distributors. The rationale was that the first generation of distributors, the oldest generation, had good, strong relationships with the Seagram management and the Bronfman family. But there was no way to insure that the next generation, the heirs to the distributors' businesses, would feel the same way. Mr. Bronfman said, "Essentially, we were trying to help our distributors become better businessmen. Other people in the industry have tried to do it without any success, but ours has been going on now for years and years, and it's something they all look forward to. And they're all very rich and important and powerful businessmen today, but they like that feeling of family that comes through at those meetings.

"We'd bring all the senior executives to some nice place, like Arizona say, and we'd bring in speakers that would be of interest to them, and we'd run seminars to help them with their business problems, things like that.

"But, really, it was about relationships. It was a way to keep the relationships strong. And now we're on the third generation of relationships."

7. Do It With Hospitality

When I sat down to interview Danny Meyer, it was clearly important to him not only to offer me a cup of coffee, but to say: "Would you like it the way I drink it?"—which was in an elegant, tall glass on a saucer.

It's important to Barbara Corcoran that every guest who walks into her corporate offices is offered a drink by the receptionist and is led to a huge walk-in refrigerator that is organized with wire shelves stocked with every cold drink imaginable.

And during my interview with him, Edgar Bronfman showed a level of graciousness and hospitality that was extraordinary: After we had seated ourselves across a table, I took out my fancy, digital mini-disc recorder with its multi-directional stereo microphone powerful enough to pick up the rumblings of my nervous stomach. I set it down between us and turned it on. It was absolutely dead as a doornail. Useless. I felt pathetic beyond belief. And I apologized profusely, and suggested that maybe I come back at another time, while thinking that, of course, I'd really blown it. . . .

Which is when he said, "We will not be defeated by technology," and had his assistant search around the office until she found an old tape recorder that was lying in a drawer somewhere. Neither she nor I could figure out how to use it, so Edgar futzed around with it himself until he figured it out. Finally he turned it on, tested it, and let me start as if nothing had happened. That's hospitality.

Like Edgar Bronfman, successful people know instinctively that in order to connect with others, you need to treat them like guests, and treat them with the importance you hope they may someday have in your life. It's a strength, not a weakness. It shows that they feel comfortable enough with themselves that they want to offer to include others in it.

It's not a particularly natural way for we American businesspeople to act. Americans seem to have a bias against hospitality, especially toward people who are more successful. We tend to get a little nasty, to feel and sometimes do things that show other people that "I don't have to suck up to you." We tend to withhold our generosity until we get what we want.

But, of course, that's childish anger. It only convinces others that we're not made of the right stuff, that we're not bred for greatness. To the degree that there's any good breeding left in the world, it's recognizable by good manners. The well-bred are always connected, they always look you in the eye, they always appear interested, they're always on time. They're always hospitable. And good manners always help you connect with others.

John Limbert, currently the Deputy Coordinator for Counterterrorism at the U.S. State Department, was one of the captives in the American embassy in Iran during the hostage crisis of 1980. He told me that he managed to get himself treated reasonably well by his captors using a very simple technique: Whenever the guards came by, he invited them into his cell as if it were his home. "I would say to them, 'Come in,' and I would proceed with classic hospitable motions. 'Please, take a seat. It's nice to see you again.' We'd go on in this way, pretending that the situation was not what it really was." He worked on being gracious and hospitable toward his captors and made them feel a connection with him. It was harder for them to act abusively toward someone who treated them graciously.

A good lesson to learn in the business world.

Limbert says, "In a similar fashion, I now always keep a dish of candy in my office. And it's surprising: I always offer somebody candy when they come in, and it always lightens the mood. It's hard to be nasty to someone who's just offered you candy."

8. If You're Not Born with Social Ease, Find It

A few years ago, when I was a senior vice president and head of corporate affairs at Prudential Securities, I reported to Wick Simmons, who was our chairman. Wick comes from the sort of pedigree that most of us imagine when we think of the world of "High Finance." His grandfather founded one of Wall Street's major brokerage houses, he grew up in Boston, summered on Nantucket, and as a youngster attended Groton. He then, of course, went on to follow in the footsteps of the six generations that preceded him and graduated from Harvard College and subsequently from the Harvard Business School.

Most of us who worked with Wick just assumed that, because of his background and the people he grew up surrounded by, doors were opened for him that were never opened for us. We all fantasized about how he must have been on family sailing trips with a former head of Goldman Sachs before he graduated college, about how he had dined several times with senior partners at Paul, Weiss, Rifkind while still in grade school, and how he spent summers at the home of a college friend whose CEO father ultimately offered Wick a six-figure job right out of school.

None of that, of course, had happened.

When I interviewed Wick for this book, he told me that, in fact, all of the people who played a role in the development of his career were strangers to him when he began. Connections just were not a part of it.

"I don't believe social connections make much of a difference. But social ease does. The important thing in business is an ability to relate socially, whether in big groups or small. It makes the task so much easier. The ability to mix with any crowd on your terms is an outgrowth of your self-confidence and that, of course, is influenced by your upbringing. To some degree, for me, it was an inherited skill: My mother and my father were both totally at ease in social situations. It came rather naturally to me. But it is also a skill that can be learned. I've seen people cultivate it. With training, anyone can learn to enter a room with assurance. When I say *assurance* what I'm talking about is not arrogance or smugness, but simply an understanding that, *yes, I can play here. . . .*"

That sort of self-confidence comes naturally to some, and for others, it takes hard work, determination, and lots and lots of practice.

Nothing breeds more quickly or with more negative impact than discomfort: If you feel uneasy and self-conscious when you're around another person, he or she will feel the tension and the relationship will suffer. The goal is to go into business situations feeling comfortable in your skin, knowing who you are and not pretending to be anyone else, and thereby making those around you feel comfortable themselves.

9. Plan Ahead

If you're someone who gets flummoxed in the moment, if you're someone who knows you don't do well at cocktail parties, if you were the kid in high school who often found himself sitting alone in the cafeteria—it's even more important to you than it is to others to plan ahead. But, in my experience with successful people, whether they're naturally gregarious or naturally shy, they plan ahead with relationship issues.

It's what David Rockefeller's card system is all about: It's about never letting yourself get into a situation in which you feel out of control or in a spot. Successful people always try to find out whom they're going to be seeing when they go to a party or a dinner or a charity function: They want to be prepared.

It's the same as what successful dieting is all about: If you come home and the only thing you have to eat is Häagen-Dazs in the freezer, you're going to eat it. You've got to have other things on hand to satisfy your hunger, or it's not going to work. You've got to plan ahead.

The same issue applies when it comes to meeting people: You never want to walk into a room cold. You need to be prepared and not be faced with a situation that may be damaging to you. The first time you look at the list of who's there should not be when you're sitting there, listening to the first speaker. You should have some idea of who's going to be there, even if it's just a list of the speakers; you should have brainstormed for yourself who else might be there, given the speakers, the industry, the host, and the attendees you already know about. You should think in advance about what you'd like to say to the people you're likely to see, whether you already know them or not.

You also can, and should, initiate a circle before you even walk in the room. Call four people you know will be at the event and plan to sit together, or plan to meet afterward for dinner or an after-dinner drink. Just knowing that they're there and that you have a plan will make you feel more comfortable.

Unless you're completely comfortable in social situations, and very few people truly are, the less that is left to on-the-spot decisions, the better.

GETTING STARTED

There's no easy way to force yourself to keep it personal—that only comes with the hard work of following a systematic plan for staying in touch.

David Rockefeller's is more complex than most people could possibly handle; Shelly Lazarus's is more instinctual than people without her natural instincts can handle. The goal is to come up with some plan that feels right for you and stick with it.

What follows are two systems that are solid, practical, and will work for most people. If one of them feels right to you, adopt it; if it doesn't, adapt it. The first system was made up for you "blues" out there. It's a budget system and will give you a structured place to start. And the second, I wrote for you "pinks." It's a diet plan. Read both and use whichever appeals to you. Or draw from both systems and make your own.

The Budget System

Whether or not you are aware of it, you are already budgeting your most precious resource: time. You are making unconscious decisions all day about whom to be in touch with and for how long

. . . and whom not to be in touch with. The goal of working on a budget is to make more of those decisions conscious, so that you can look at the time you are spending and spend it wisely.

The first step is the same as with any other budget. You need to be able to answer the question: "Where the hell does it all go, anyway?" The only way to answer that question is to write down how you are spending it. In this case, you need to determine how you are spending the time you use in relating to other people. Only by writing it down are life's little mysteries revealed. Sometimes you don't want to know the answer (like how much my three-cappuccino-a-day habit is costing). Just remember that the truth is power.

What do you write down? Take a couple of days the first week and write down all the activities you are involved in currently. Include activities that relate to potential business relationships and note how long you are spending on each.

You might want to set up a few columns for categories first. Then put a little dot for each ten minutes. If you need motivation, pretend you are a lawyer and someone is going to pay you for it.

Here are some of the activities you may want to track:

- How much time sending and responding to e-mail?

- How much time on the phone?

- How much time on the phone *while* doing e-mail?

- How much time talking at the water cooler, grabbing a smoke with someone, or just hanging out in one another's space?

- How much time at breakfast? Lunch? Dinner? Drinks? Coffee?

- How much time after working hours? Weekends?

- How much time in one-to-one meetings? (You can count larger ones only if you really believe that the meetings create relationship potential, which is rare.)

How much time did you get for each day? Multiply an average day by five, or, if you want a more accurate picture, track for a week. My guess is that you have at least ten or fifteen hours and probably much more for your people activities.

You can see how easy it is to get to 30 percent of your time (at a minimum) being spent on relationships.

The second week, pick a couple of sample days and track not activities, but people. Keep a diary, or go back through your agenda at the end of a day. Don't include every chance encounter, but think about the people who are significant to your career, or potentially so. List them all. Now go through the list and divide them into three categories.

Category One is board potential. As you will recall from Principle Four, these are the people whose values you share and with whom you want to grow and to whom you have something to offer.

Category Two are people whom you like and whose role requires your attention. These are the people you were thinking about in Principle Two, where we talked about role. To some degree, they are given to you by an organization, like business cards. They are there and you need to make those relationships work.

Category Three are the ones you were thinking about in Principle Six. They are the people who take up your energy: either garden variety users, underperformers, or just plain someone who you believe, for whatever reason, to be your enemy.

Can't figure out what category someone is in? Here's a quick tip. Imagine you have caller I.D. Visualize a specific name on the phone. Category One is the person you would be proud to tell other people you have on your personal board or would want on your team pursuing a new business opportunity, no matter what it was. Category Two is the person whose name you see and your first thought is the task you are working on together, not any particular thoughts about the person. Category Three is the person whose name you see and then . . . your heart sinks.

Once you have the list divided by category, use the same dot tracking system for every ten minutes. Don't consider every name, just put a dot by the category. Ten minutes for Category One when you have a good talk with someone you respect about a future business project. The twenty minutes you spend on a tirade with a Category Two about a Category Three is energy you're spending on a Category Three, and you should put a dot in the Category Three column.

As with activities, figure out how much time a week you are spending on each category. Of the 30 percent (or more) of your business life you are spending on relationships, how much is an investment—Category One . . . and how much isn't—Category Three.

Set your own budget. You know what you can afford and I don't. But I would suggest that spending 80 percent of your time on Category One is a whole lot smarter than on Category Three.

Once you know where you are spending it, look at how. Is most of your relationship time e-mail? Consider cutting back 25 percent and spending that time face-to-face if possible, or on the phone if not. How much of your relationship time is in ten-minute increments? Remember that chunks of time are more powerful and try to schedule at least one longer activity (lunch, golf, or shoe shopping, my favorite) with someone you value.

The Relationship Diet Plan

Okay, for all of you who couldn't get into tracking or categories, here's an easier to swallow metaphor, the relationship diet plan.

It's just a way of thinking. This diet may be Atkins and you need Pritikin, but take a quick spin through it for some inspiration on how to get relationship variety into your day.

Dr. Ronna's Rules for Healthy Relationship Consumption

1. *Eat Tons of Veggies.* Got a boss? If so, they are the vegetables of this food pyramid, and this time they're at the bottom: They're the base. You need to fortify yourself with them more than any

other food group for obvious reasons: They pay you, they can make your work life easier or harder, they can fire you.

But even more important for your ultimate career success is that they most likely know a lot more about your profession than you do. And they can, if willing to do so, teach you ways to advance in your career.

Bosses can introduce you to other important people in your field, they can lead you toward the more exciting clients and projects, they can help you solve problems. Pound for pound, they carry more value than any other type of person you'll come in contact within your career.

As you put together your career eating plan, don't skimp on bosses. Just like vegetables, try to have frequent small servings every day.

2. *Go for Grains.* Grains are the people who make your work life easier, who do what you do, or who are essential to getting your task done.

They are the colleagues in your organization who are at your level or below, people who work on different aspects of the same projects you do, or joint venture partners.

They are the people who give you energy, who fuel your ideas, who not only nourish you but fill you up. They are the ones you see every day, who work alongside you, who form the solid core of your daily routine.

Because they're a staple, it's easy to take them for granted. Whole-grain toast doesn't seem very festive—until it isn't there.

3. *Watch the Dairy.* You need dairy products to build strong bones, and in your career think of the people who advise you as dairy: lawyers, accountants, financial advisors, risk managers, consultants. These people have roles that are important in your career, but need to be taken in moderation. After all, too much dairy can be hard to digest.

Think about it: If you start to rely too strongly on the advice of lawyers, or accountants, or any advisor for that matter, you lose the broader picture. By definition, their focus is narrower than yours.

Dairy people's job and agenda are to protect you. That means that there are certain kinds of risks that it's their business to advise you against—particularly, relationship risks. They've seen so many relationships go bad over deals that they're cautious. They're always thinking of the worst-case scenario.

You have a deal with someone and then you introduce inter-mediaries into the mix and there's a chance that someone will get upset. In addition, lawyers are paid to make things specific, which can slow things down and stress primary relationships.

Relationships that are centered around doing deals can feel like Saturday night; lawyers make it feel like Sunday morning. Your job is to work out a good way to get through Sunday mornings. My friend Tank has a system for this. He will shake hands over the general deal logistics and let the lawyers, accountants, etc., talk to one another. He does the conceptual work and then lets the dairy team manage the details. If a problem arises, he waits until it comes back up the food chain and addresses it with the first per-son he made the deal with.

The other thing to watch is if you're using dairy out of habit or out of real need. There are some trust-based relationships that I have where I make a deal and I don't use Larry, my incredibly able lawyer (much to his dismay). Our deal is that he's willing to honor my relationship values unless he sees something that really makes him uncomfortable. When that happens, I listen.

If you ingest dairy to the extreme, you'll lose the ability to keep things moving along. *You* have the larger perspective on your career path. Make sure to keep it that way.

4. *Eat Moderate Amounts of Protein Frequently.* Proteins are your revenue sources: clients, accounts, customers. And, of course, you need enough of them to sustain yourself. They are a high source of your energy and your business strength.

But you need to make sure that they are of a high quality and carry a big punch. Too many, too fast, and you'll get fat before you know it. Proteins are the hardest to digest. They take the most effort, they overwhelm the other nutrients; too much is bad for your kidneys.

It's hard to stop yourself from overindulging in protein—after all, it's where all your strength comes from. But be aware: If you don't consume in moderation, if you take on too many revenue sources too quickly, you won't be able to digest them. They'll throw your system off balance. You'll end up leaving them, and you, unfulfilled and looking for sustenance elsewhere.

5. *Have Limited Amounts of Fruit.* Think of people who work in the communications world as fruit: the commentators, the media, the trend trackers, the analysts, the Internet. They're a quick, sweet burst of energy. They keep things moving. They're good for you because they can give you information. But remember, they're mostly sugar: They burn up quickly. Best to balance them with other nutrients.

6. *Avoid Alcohol.* Alcohol can be fun, it can be seductive, it can make a good time feel better or make a tough time feel easier. But it can overwhelm you if you're not careful.

There are people you come in contact with in your professional career who will take the role of alcohol in your nutrition plan: They are the ones who carry big emotional charges—the ones who push your buttons, who get under your skin in either a good way or a bad way. The people you think about more than you should, the people whom you obsess about, the ones you want either to kill, sleep with, or both.

Jane Grenley is a Senior Vice President for development in a toy manufacturing company. She manages a large creative staff who come up with new toy and game ideas day in and day out. While it sounds like fun, in Jane's staff, like in any creative team, tempers can run very high—and the stress level of managing such a group causes Jane many sleepless nights.

The one thing that causes her more sleepless nights, though, is

Leslie Quinn, the Senior Vice President of corporate communications, who is her colleague at the company. Both women report to the CEO.

Jane, by nature, is slightly reserved and very smart. Leslie is wildly extroverted, incredibly funny and charming, and says whatever is on her mind, whether or not she has thought about it first. She often unwittingly insults members of the creative team with her off-the-cuff comments about their work. And, because she is fun to be around and is often the center of attention, the CEO enjoys her company, and he often seems to be giving her more than her fair share of attention.

Leslie makes Jane's blood boil. Jane frets over how close Leslie seems to be with the CEO, she is quickly angered over what she perceives as slights in Leslie's comments about the creative team's work, and she spends way too much of her time thinking of what she should have said in response to Leslie at corporate meetings. And the thing that Jane finds it hardest to acknowledge is that she finds herself drawn to Leslie's gregarious personality as well.

To Jane, Leslie is alcohol, and she needs to be completely avoided or taken in tiny doses. Leslie has the power to intoxicate Jane: Her acts go right to Jane's head, and they make Jane do things she might not otherwise do, things that could prove embarrassing. Jane has had to stop herself several times from saying bitchy things to the CEO about Leslie, or from attacking Leslie personally at meetings—both of which make her look unprofessional and petty.

Jane has to have the discipline of a twelve-step lifetime member as far as Leslie is concerned. She must avoid her as much as possible, and when she has no choice, she must keep her lips dry. She has to remember that indulging even once could be a big mistake.

7. *Strictly Limit Your Intake of Fats.* Fats are fun. They taste good, they go down easily, they add richness and pleasure. Too much is not good for you, but dammit, we just can't stop ourselves once we start.

In a career, fats are the people we like to waste time with. Our office buddies, our e-mail pals, our industry friends. The people who call you to gossip and have nothing really to say, the people who have the time to send you endless e-mails with "thoughts of the day" or, God help us, e-chain letters. The office people we go to lunch with just to complain.

Our relationships with these people feel good. They're soothing, they go down easily, they're comforting.

They are not as charged as the alcoholic ones, but they can be just as bad for you. They dull you, they make you fat and lazy. They soften the edges. They fill you up and don't leave room for the things you really need.

8. *Eat Small Amounts of Sugar.* These are the people who are paid to be nice to you.

People in the old days called sugar people "yes-men." Most people have "yes" moments, especially when they think you need it. Here's a tale of one of mine.

I was getting ready for an interview on *60 Minutes* with Mike Wallace where I was the representative for my old company. It wasn't a happy story and I figured the least I could do was look good. When my makeup and hair were done, the woman that did my hair gushed on and on for about fifteen minutes about how great my makeup looked. When I showed up at the studio, Mike asked me if I wanted them to do my makeup, which should have told me something, but didn't. I said no. After all, the woman who did my hair said I looked great, even though a small voice inside was telling me that the tiny clumps of fake eyelashes looked reminiscent of Miss Piggy.

The segment turned out fine: *60 Minutes* wasn't too happy and my company wasn't too unhappy. I looked terrible. Awful. In fact, I've never received so many calls from people saying, "Ronna, what happened?" What happened was that I listened to someone who told me what I wanted to hear instead of what I needed to hear.

Sugar people are *supposed* to make you feel good. They tell you what you want to hear, they do what you tell them to do, they don't argue. They want you to be nice to them, they want you to buy what they offer, they want your approval. And they'll do whatever they need to do in order to get it.

And you know what? In moderation, that's fine. It feels good to be kissed-up to, and what's the harm? As long as we are sure that these people aren't lying or cheating or pulling a fast one on us, the only harm is in the time it takes. So focus on task and limit the time. Get a little sugar rush to keep your energy up. Just don't kid yourself into believing that Hershey's Kisses are the ideal lunch. Especially before a big game.

Making the System Work for You

Once you have set time in your schedule for relationship building, you'll be amazed at how you naturally find ways to get rid of the clutter. It's like the way that new parents, who never think they can manage to keep their career intact when an infant arrives, somehow manage to find time for the important things at work. When you set the priorities and have a deep understanding of what is important to you, you'll naturally leave behind the unimportant things and gravitate toward the things that make you grow.

If my proposed budgeting system or diet plan doesn't work for you, build your own. Keep tinkering with it to make it better. It's there for you, to free you, to act as a guide and a memory. But it won't get you very far if your heart isn't in the right place, if you're not doing battle with the demons that keep you isolated.

I started this chapter talking about the systems that brokers have for "contact management." Think about this, though: Those systems are readily available to every one of the brokers working at the big brokerage firms. Why is it that some of them make millions, far outpacing the rest?

Here's the difference:

One night I got a cold call from a broker. He was touting a stock, and I told him I wasn't interested. In fact, at that time, I worked for a rival firm and government regulations forbade me from trading with someone else. I told him this. He kept talking.

Frustrated, I said, "What are you doing? Why are you still trying to get me to a seminar?" And he said these immortal words: "Because I want to have a relationship with you." A classic example of the right words and the wrong music.

Contrast that with one of the top producers at Prudential Securities when I was there: Let's call him Abe Greenberg. Abe was a self-described "little guy." He was short, unimposing, didn't wear flashy suits. What he did have were families—dozens of families— for whom he had handled the investments for three generations. And he did it by spending all his energy on getting to know them, understanding them, concentrating on what made them comfortable. He would focus on the small things, like what kind of language made people nervous.

Abe did not look like a master of the universe. But he was. His ability to sincerely think of the other person, put his own need for recognition behind, and to maintain relationships made him one of the most successful brokers in the business.

It doesn't matter how good your system of reminders is if what it reminds you to do is something that feels insubstantial and insincere to the other people. The important thing is to take the risk and to make it personal, to give freely of yourself and to be open and intimate. Relationships evolve only when people know and love the real you.

And the only way they're going to get to know the real you is if you reach out and maintain contact.

Give Yourself Time to Win

"Successful people understand that their own energy is a precious resource, and they never waste it."
—MORT MEYERSON

NOW THAT I'VE OVERWHELMED YOU WITH ALL OF THE SYSTEMS SUCcessful people use to maintain and deepen their relationships, I bet you're still wondering how they find the time to do it all. And more important, I bet you're wondering how you are going to do it all. Where is the time in your day to make those extra calls to potential board members or write a personal note to that woman you recently connected with at a party?

After talking to many of the successful people, I, too, was a bit intimidated by their ability to make it personal with so many people, so I began listening for how they make time. And as I suspected, they don't make time by adding hours to every day to attend to things like their personal board members. Successful people know their goals, prioritize their emotional and relationship investments, and, most important, keep a long-term perspective.

ROME WAS NOT BUILT IN A DAY

Successful people know that relationships take time. They are built slowly, by multiple exposures, by the slow growth of trust and of mutual respect and a realization of shared values, over many months—at least—and often over several years. They know there's no way around that.

Real intensity comes from shared experience, it comes from the sort of intimacy that is only possible after shared pain, shared triumph, and shared disappointments. Winners understand that the only way to build dependable and profound trust-based relationships is to stay for the duration.

But in today's marketplace, that's tough to do. We're an instant-gratification society, especially in the business world. If a movie isn't in the top five in its first weekend, it's written off as a failure. Books and records are given, maybe, three weeks. If a start-up company's stock price doesn't climb continuously quarter to quarter, analysts give it a failing grade. If a new chairman, president, even department head doesn't turn around a company in his or her first six months on the job, good-bye Charlie. We've changed from a society of investors to a society of day traders, looking for an instant payoff, a quick killing, and we're more and more willing to discard the things that don't grant us that fast payoff.

Call me old-fashioned, but the "instant" attitude has its limits. And if you do call me old-fashioned, call dozens of successful people old-fashioned, too, because in their estimation, real winning and major wealth and true success come from sticking it out for the long term.

Ken Langone told me that he doesn't keep a stock-ticker anywhere in his sight. "It's counterproductive to the way I do business. I'm not in it to make a fast buck and get out, I'm in it to create value over the long haul. I want my investments to last five, ten, fifteen years. I'm going for the big returns, and the big returns come over time."

And the same is true with people. Langone went on, "Do you know what the average length of time is that people work for this company? Eighteen or nineteen years. It's unbelievable today, but it's true. We believe in people for the long term, we believe in our investments for the long term. We want us all to come out winners when the game is over, and to have a nice, long, successful run together.

"Some people come to invest with my company and I tell them, 'Please, don't; if you want results in ninety days, we can't promise that. If you're in it for the short term, go elsewhere. But if you hope to have superior investment results, leave it with us for five years or more. Then we have a chance to give you those results.'

"People who make serious money—look at the Forbes list or any other measure—and you'll see that it's people who take the long view. Real masses of wealth are created not by traders, but by investors."

And people who know how to get the most out of their relationships have the same viewpoint.

There's no question that it was easier in the old days. Phyllis Grann told me that she thought relationship management is much more difficult today in publicly held companies. "The worst thing that's happened to American business is running companies quarter to quarter for the analysts." Losing the long-term perspective creates a short-term mentality that ultimately can hurt value rather than improve it. When you invest in your own company, you must do what you believe in for the long-term health and robust growth of the business, and that is quite often something that is not in the best interest of the short-term investor.

When you look at the long view in your business relationships, you're looking at creating the trust-based relationships that some people think of almost as a family: the ten-, fifteen-, twenty-year relationships that give you the solid foundation you need for true success. And when you work in a publicly-held environment, you have to work very hard to keep mindful of the fact that paying attention to those long-term responsibilities may well pay off better than listening to the short-term requirements of Wall Street.

Don Keough, Chairman of Allen & Company, Inc., said to me, "Unless you have a long-term view, I don't care whether you're a new on-line company or whether you're an old-line company, you're just not going to be around. And young people who don't realize that are going to have trouble as they organize their own businesses in the years to come. Over the long term, you can't be successful without developing sound relationships."

Long-term success requires long-term attention to relationships: to customers, to colleagues, to employees, and to clients. It cannot be done with a quarter-to-quarter perspective. You need to consider it your life's work.

And a way to do that, regardless of the values of the corporation you may work in, is to think of yourself as your own privately held company.

Remember that, ultimately, your career is your own privately owned business, Me, Inc. Your relationships, you hope, are there *forever*. Even if you're stuck in circumstances in which the emphasis is on nothing more than the next ninety days, you have to take every step you can to make sure that you're protecting yourself for the long term. Let's say you work for a company that's not so wisely run: in a company where nobody takes the view longer than the end of the next fiscal quarter. Remember this: Life is going to move on. Ten years from now, the second quarter of 2001 is going to be a distant memory. No one is going to remember a dip in the stock price. But people will remember if you were there for them, or if you turned your back on them.

Not Right Now

Successful people recognize that some relationships are not meant for the present. But that does not mean that they say, "No, never." Successful people say, "No, thank you, not right now," which does two things: It saves them time in the present to focus on the relationships that can help them achieve their current goals, and it gives them the opportunity to return to that person, whom they may need at a later date.

Julie Daum told me a cautionary tale about a woman who said, "No, never." This executive flew down to meet with a client of Julie's, the CEO of a big company, who was interested in considering the woman for their board. They talked for several hours, she said she'd think about it and get back to him in a month. She was being pursued for several boards at the time.

She never called him back. Julie Daum logged about ten calls into her office before she got through, and finally she was able to say to her, 'You flew all the way down there to meet with him, a phone call will close the loop. You never know when you might want to call this guy again.' She never did it, never called. Julie Daum couldn't figure it out. This woman had spent a day to fly down and meet and talk about this seat and all she had to do was say, 'I'm sorry, I have a very high regard for you and your company, but my schedule doesn't allow me to accept. It was lovely to meet you, please stay in touch.' Because she didn't find the time to make a thirty-second phone call she has a major company and a powerful CEO thinking she's a jerk. Why?

As Julie pointed out, "She clearly has no understanding of relationships. All she knew was that she was being pursued, that she had the power. She was only seeing the way things stood on that very day, not thinking six months into the future when she might need that CEO for something. It's shortsighted and incredibly self-destructive. You just know that woman is going to need that company some day, and what they'll remember is that she didn't have the decency to call them back."

When you ignore people, or don't follow though on a relationship issue, you risk not only missing out on an opportunity to build a closer bond, you flirt with making an enemy. You can be fairly certain that the chairman who waited and waited for the phone call from the non-responsive board candidate will not, six months later, be inclined to take her call on another matter. And this time the subject might be a matter of extreme importance to her.

Liz Smith says, "I try very hard to do all those things you're supposed to do: to answer every piece of mail, to pick it up, make a decision about it, dispatch it. You know, I try. Sometimes I just attack it and work on it for hours and get everything back in twenty-four hours.

"Then other times weeks can go by, and I just can't get mail answered. I can't make a decision, or other things just come along and ride right over it and this can go on until it's too late to answer, or I've missed a deadline or something. These things happen.

"But when it does, I make sure, when I've got my sanity back, to write a note to whomever I overlooked. *'I'm sorry that I didn't respond to your request. We were just in a big tizzy here and couldn't write about it. So write to me about something else, and I'll try to do it another time.'* Something like that. It really makes a difference and saves your bacon."

Liz knows that to leave someone hanging, to leave any request unanswered, is rude and makes enemies. A simple response, even if it's only an apology after the fact, leaves room for further communication.

Tom Quick of Quick & Reilly/Fleet Securities, Inc., finds missed opportunities just as serious a mistake.

"I find it really silly that most people, if they meet someone at a cocktail party or other social occasion, and the person says, 'Give me a call,' they let it drop and don't follow up on it. I think most people are just too insecure, too uncomfortable. They make excuses to themselves: *'Oh, he was just being polite, he doesn't really want me to call him.'* And sometimes that's the case. But how do you know unless you try?

"And, sure, if you try several times and don't get a call back, get the picture and move on. But if someone was sincere about the opportunity, and you drop it, you've only got yourself to blame."

I thought about this issue a lot during the writing of this book because it was in my face as I pursued successful people for interviews.

What I was looking for in the selection process were people who were clearly successful on a performance basis: e.g., had run big businesses, were at the top of their field, perhaps had made a lot of money, and were also people who I had some reason to believe handled relationships well. That component was harder to judge, of course, and I chose my candidates either by things I had read about them that indicated that they were good at relationships or because I had heard good things about them from someone I trusted.

I ended up with quite a good batting average: Most of the people I wanted to interview, I got. But not everybody. I found that the way in which people declined revealed their relationship skills.

The best no I got was from Jack Welch at General Electric. I had written him a blind request asking for an interview, which described the subject matter of the book. And the letter I got back, though it was a no, came quickly, was polite, and indicated that he had seriously considered the request.

I also got a fabulous no from Richard Branson of Virgin—whose office first sent me a note saying that they were swamped and would be getting back to me shortly; and then they followed up with a call saying that, sorry, this just was not going to work for Mr. Branson.

I only had one incident of someone who was blatantly offensive. The Man Who Is a Famous Movie Mogul, who, also, is quite a well-known name in his industry and someone who I had good reason to believe would be responsive to the book. We also had someone in common, and that person indicated to me that Famous Mogul would be willing to talk to me.

So I sent him a gracious letter, and I got a call from someone who sounded like they were still on the high school drama squad and with the same bored and imperious tone I was told "Mr. Mogul does not grant interviews." Which was patently absurd, Mr. Mogul is interviewed in the press every other day.

> "You don't want to be a discarder of people. You engage people in a variety of ways, but once you engage, then you want to be fair and reasonable. What's reasonable mean? It means understanding human beings, that they'll do things that will offend you from time to time, they'll make mistakes, they won't always be right, they aren't always going to be at your pace, they aren't always going to agree with what you think."
>
> —KEN LANGONE

Still, I tried to be polite and asked, does Mr. Mogul remember that he told our mutual friend that he'd be willing to do this? I was literally screamed at: *"Did you hear what I said? No interviews."*

Does he care that I was treated so badly? Of course not.

But the point is this: He *should* care. Not about me, but about the big picture. If I'm being treated this way, others are, too. And you just never know how these things will come back to get you. Sure, it doesn't matter to Mr. Mogul what I think, but it will matter if one of the fund managers who controls tens of thousands of shares of his parent company's stock feels the same way I do.

It didn't take Jack Welch or his staff any more time to respond to me in a way that left me feeling cared for and respected than it took Mr. Mogul to respond in a way that left me feeling abused. Jack Welch says, "Not right now," leaving the possibility of relationship open for the future. That allows him to pick it up again whenever he likes.

No Time for the Pain

With their long-term perspective, successful people also realize that mistakes are not life-threatening catastrophes, but merely bumps along the long road. They don't waste time and energy mourning their mistakes or obsessing about things that don't work out. They don't dwell. They don't beat themselves up over mistakes. They learn what they can, they see what was useful, and they move on to other projects and goals.

On this subject, the interviews echoed one another: Michael Goldstein told me, "Probably the most important thing for a business person is to fail." Dick Beattie, Chairman of the Executive

Committee at Simpson Thacher & Bart-lett told me, "I never think it's a mistake. You can misjudge people, and people can disappoint you, but that doesn't make it a mistake." Lauren Shuler Don-ner said, "People make mistakes. I've made mistakes. I've turned down mov-ies. I've turned down scores of movies, one of which was a mistake. Can't help it."

They don't dwell on the pain. Not the pain of disappointment, not the pain of rejection, not the pain of losing.

And it's not that things don't go wrong for them; indeed, I heard bloodcurdling stories throughout the interviews of re-lationships that went horribly wrong, of brutal betrayals and lost friendships and severed partnerships. There was a litany

> "I'm not saying that I'm not hurt when things fail. Movies fail, books fail. Everybody's had failures, and it feels awful. I mourn, I grieve, and I move on. Physically, mentally, psychically, fiscally—every way. I just move on and get over it.
>
> "And I certainly don't hold a grudge. What's the point? Acid corrodes the vessel in which it resides—and hate is acidic. It hurts you, it's unproductive, you have to just get away from it and move on."
>
> —DAVID BROWN

of stories of things that have gone awry. But what I never heard from the successful people, as they told me those stories, was lingering regret. And that marked an enormous difference between the successful people I talked to for this book and the unsuccess-ful people who have come to me for counsel. Unsuccessful people dwell on the pain: They play it over in their minds day in and day out, they think about the things they could have done, or should have done, they obsess over the opportunities that they lost, or the things they should have said, or the call they never made. They flagellate themselves mercilessly over any failure or loss, and the blame and guilt that they carry around with them is often stifling and holds them back from future endeavors.

Successful people, on the other hand, don't overindulge in self-blame. That's not to say they're delusional or irresponsible. No, they are well aware of their own errors in judgment and of the wrong paths they've taken. They simply understand that having

> "**S**ome people have had highly successful careers. They've been successful in everything. And because I had a career like that, I understand that that prepares you for failure. It doesn't prepare you for success. And so I'd much rather find somebody who was successful most of the time, but who has had failure because they've experienced it, because they learned from it. I mean, it's like steel. Steel is made harder in a furnace by hammering, not by sitting in a corner somewhere."
> —MORT MEYERSON

some lapses is part of the picture, and they move on.

It's not that they don't feel the pain. They do. They feel it intensely. It's that they learn from it. They don't live with it until the day they die. And they never let the experience of pain hold them back from taking a similar chance again.

Mort Meyerson told me, "It's a willingness to give it its place and experience it. You have to experience it, not be above it. Vulnerability is one step away from this, but important. You have to make yourself vulnerable in order to be able to get to the place to feel the pain. So that's like a transitional step in there. But you have to actually experience the pain to understand what other people go through and what they're experiencing to be able to relate to them. Otherwise, you're lost."

The other key is not letting a loss or a failure impede you from taking future action. Successful people learn from their mistakes, they use what they can to help make better decisions the next time, and they put the unpleasantness behind them.

Shelly Lazarus told me: "We're going to make mistakes, we're going to do it wrong. You have to give up the requirement to be perfect. You know, I think the courage to make mistakes is the most underrated trait in all business leaders. And it seems to be particularly a problem for women.

> "**I** always start a meeting by telling the mistakes I made in the last two or three weeks, to show people how fallible I am."
> —BERNIE MARCUS

"I don't know where this came from in me, but I was always okay with making mistakes, I knew it was part of the game."

Shelly had one of those epiphanies—it happened early on in her career. She worked for a fabulous man named Charlie Fredricks, who was a wonderful, spontaneous human being with a great values system.

Shelly was in Charlie's office one day when a media planner came in who started running around his office in circles—*literally* running in circles. Shelly had never seen anyone do that before. The media planner was hysterical. It was in the days of big mainframe computers, and the planner had an important meeting at Lever Brothers that started at two o'clock. She was supposed to present the media plan for one of their big brands for the next year, but the computer was down, and she just couldn't get the plan out of it.

It was now 1:15. The computer was not going to get fixed. So she kept running around in circles until Charlie Fredricks moved to stand in her path. He blocked her way. He grabbed her by the shoulders, and he shook her. When she stopped long enough to look into his eyes, he said to her, "What do you think they're going to do to you? Take away your children?"

I laughed when Shelly told me this and asked her if those were his exact words. She responded, "Yes. I'll never forget that. Whatever is going on, no matter how difficult a situation is, I think: 'What are they going to do, take away my children?' I mean, sure, I can get fired. But I know that I can get another job if I do. How bad could it be? And once you realize that, it's okay to be brave."

One of the things that makes Shelly Lazarus so successful is her ability to go toward the pain, not to avoid it. Successful people are not afraid of being hurt—they know that the hurt will not kill them—and, in fact, they know that without the hurt, their business life and

> "**S**ometimes you get to a point where you just can't be involved with a person. It's too difficult, things just aren't right. You just move on: You never bad-mouth or slander the person, that's wasted energy and energy that, in fact, makes you look bad with the person hearing it."
> —MICHAEL GOLDSTEIN

> "Enduring character is built with adversity and builds over time. It isn't something you just acquire."
> —NEIL LIVINGSTONE

possibilities will be pretty lackluster. They know that to fear the pain would be to wallow in insecurity and would undermine any hope of real success.

Bernie Marcus told me about his mistake philosophy, which I loved. "Making mistakes is a great learning experience. I've always said the same thing. If you tell me in advance and I know it's going to happen, then when it goes down, I say, 'Hey listen, I was your partner, I knew what was happening. Because I was your partner, we both made a mistake. Come on, let's move on with life and let's correct it. . . . ' The companies that fail typically fail because number one, they don't recognize a mistake; and number two, they don't fix it. In most companies, they recognize a mistake, they're afraid of the consequences of being caught, and therefore they cover it up constantly. And all of their energy now goes into covering it up instead of moving on to other things.

"When you recognize you've made a mistake and you're able to say, 'Whew! That was dumb. Let me correct it, and let's get on,' it takes one-tenth the energy. And whenever you correct the mistake, it always ends up being better than it was before as opposed to the companies that make the same mistake over and over and over again because nobody is willing to stand up and say, 'This is dumb.' "

> "You know, the best relationships I've made in my life were people that everybody else gave up on: Bernie Marcus and Arthur Blank. They were fired, thrown on the streets, out of work. Bernie called me looking for a job. I said screw a job, we're gonna start a business."
> —KEN LANGONE

Jean Hamilton told me a story about another executive who knew how to make mistakes work for him instead of against him. "When I was first working, I had a situation in which I had to deliver some bad news to my boss. The two of us and my boss's boss were all staying at the same hotel. That morning I saw my boss's boss first in the lobby. When I told him the news, he said,

'OK, let's go tell your boss together.' That meant the world to me and cemented a loyalty that never wavered. It is a lesson I have tried to apply. After all, if we are partners, we are in it together through the tough times."

With their long-term perspective, successful people realize that it's just a matter of time before we all make a mistake. So instead of being paralyzed and isolated by them, they acknowledge their mistakes to others, ask for help, learn from them, and move on.

Maybe Later

Another result of successful people's long-term perspective is that they make sure their good-byes always leave room for another hello. They understand that the world of business, and certainly any one industry, is a small one, and they make sure to leave their doors, if not wide open, at least ajar.

Linda Srere told me, "Good leaders can analyze a situation and know when not to put their people into it. Then they say good-bye. But the 'good good-bye' is one that can be said with grace and dignity, so you can leave successfully and without burning bridges."

> "You always want to leave on good terms, which means saying good-bye in a way that leaves you at peace. Sometimes I ask myself, 'If I were on a plane dropping suddenly from forty thousand feet, could I think about this and still be okay with it?'"
> —MARTY EVANS

She told me a story about a company they were pitching, and it was at a time when they were getting to pitch for a lot of businesses and were doing quite well. So her group went to their offices and made a big presentation, and she just didn't get the right feeling in the room. She knew this wasn't going to be the right fit.

"I called our prospect after the presentation and I said, 'You know, I just don't think this is a fit. I don't think it's going to work.' She agreed, and we were out of the pitch.

"I followed up with a note telling the prospect that I thought she showed great leadership and really knew what was best for her business. Two weeks later, when she was down to choosing between two agencies, I called her again to offer her any advice she might need. I touched base again when she chose her agency and then once more when the campaign broke.

"You always want to treat people the way you'd expect to be treated. It's just the right thing to do. And, you never know when that person might show up in your life again. In fact, the prospect that I mentioned is now an executive at one of our clients. It can never hurt to treat somebody with dignity and respect."

Parker Ladd said, "You never drop the ball because you never know when you may need to pick it up again five years later."

And acclaimed television and film producer David Brown told me, "You've got to say good-bye in such a way that it's not a final good-bye, that you just don't know, that if you feel like saying hello again, you have that option. Things change, and at some point you may want to reevaluate the reasons you parted with someone. Think about it: There must have been something that brought you together with that person initially that is just as important as the reason you chose to say good-bye. And maybe you'll want to go back and address that positive feeling again.

"My partner Richard Zanuck and I parted years ago, but here we are back making pictures again together. If something was once good, it's not good-bye forever."

Stay at the Table

Giving yourself time to win is the same in relationships as in the market. In Las Vegas (and in gambling in general), there is a cowboy style of investing, which means that your ability to win is limited by how long you are able to keep playing. I learned this lesson at a fairly young age. On the advice of someone close to me, my dad invested heavily in commodities options. Much later I learned that was a kind of investing that should have come with a label: "Kids, don't try this at home."

While the tip he got was smart, it was ill-timed. With large paper losses mounting by the day, Dad chose to take his losses and move on. His loss was considerable. If he had been able to afford to stay in, he would have made a lot of money, but he couldn't afford the time.

The point isn't that Dad should have stayed in the market. It's that when you are investing in people, you *can* choose to stay in the market. You are investing time and energy, which can be more valuable than money. But often the decision to stay with it, to let the market adjust, and perhaps to gently move in your favor, doesn't require more of an investment than the decision to put off having your agenda met immediately.

My friend David Metcalf explained it to me another way. He was talking about Aldo Papone, then on the board of American Express. Once, when David went to Aldo for advice, Aldo told him, "Just stay at the table. Once you walk away, you lose the chance that the deal will be done. You lose the opportunity to create value."

How you handle the things that are difficult—mistakes, disappointments, disagreements (about ideas or money)—determines the strength of business relationships. The strongest business relationships aren't the ones that are never stressed. Good times make for business buddies, but not board members. The strongest business relationships are the ones that can stretch to accommodate disagreements and then snap back, instead of snapping.

It takes time to figure out how to resolve disagreements in a business relationship. Because we are all so busy and because large organizations tend to have cultures based on minimizing confrontation, the tendency is to either avoid addressing tough issues or to avoid the person with whom you're having them. In most relationships, that's fine. As readers of my first book know, I'm not in favor of wholesale sharing of emotion in the workplace, unlike a former Gestalt therapist who told me after a workshop I'd run that she thought it was important that her boss understand how she truly felt every day about performing the tasks that made up her job.

But the only way to know if you have a potential board-level relationship is to put it to the test—deliver honest information directly and try to hang in there long enough to see if it is possible to work it through. When you make the decision to walk away instead of to work it out, it means you will never know if this was someone who was worth having on your side long after today's dispute fades from memory.

Remember, no one is perfect at this; the point is to strive to be. As I've worked on this book, I, too, have had my moments with everyone I'm close to in my business life. There have been disagreements about money, policies, terms, direction, implicit promises, and intentions; I've had moments of feeling frustrated, neglected, injured, and occasionally abused. And those moments are with the people I like, who I believe like me as well.

I can't say that I enjoy those moments, or that you should, or that successful people do. I can say that what I've learned from the successful people I talked to is that the decision to allow those moments to happen, and to stick it out, is the only way to develop relationships with depth. And relationships with depth are the only ones that you can really rely on, especially with your personal board of directors.

When you believe you're playing with another winner, the extra time you spend staying at the table usually turns out to be a small investment compared to the potential gains.

PRINCIPLE 9

Do Deals Based on Relationships

"We are all seeking someone to buy our shares, and so what you're doing is preparing to ask people to participate in your offering. So if you're asking people to participate in your offering, then you want to make sure you have a maximum value, and the way you get it is the same process as any other offering, which involves sets of relationships."

—SUZANNE JAFFE

WE'VE TALKED A LOT ABOUT OTHER PEOPLE. IT'S TIME TO TALK MORE explicitly about you. There are a lot of reasons why you work, but a safe bet is that chief among them is money. Perhaps one of the reasons you're reading this book is that you want to make more money than you do now.

Let's go back to the marketplace, the world of buyers and sellers. Whether you are selling companies to investors, cocoa beans to a chocolate factory, or Brie from that stall in Gourdes, you go through at least three steps. First, you obtain or create something of value. Second, you get the word out to potential buyers about what you're offering. Third, you strike a deal with one of them. Those three steps complete the process of bringing a product or service to market. Now that we're talking about money, and marketing, I can't resist putting my consultant's hat on for a while to tell you what this cycle of bringing a product to market means to you and how relationships will help you do it better.

Be forewarned that this chapter is a little different from the others because now we're concentrating not just on relationships but on what relationships can do—maximize the rewards of your work life. If you're on a hot streak, these tips will help you keep the heat longer. If you're on a cold streak, this will help you reset your career thermometer.

Let's start with the basics. Over the course of your working life, no matter what other products or services you bring to the market, one stands out: you. You are constantly bringing Me, Inc., to market and you always want the best deal possible. At any given time that deal may be a raise, a new job, funding, landing a big project, getting a big promotion, a bigger expense account, more people reporting to you, or the corner office that comes with a lap pool.

Now, if you are like most people in pursuit of that goal, you focus on the third step of the product to market cycle, striking the deal.

You use every bit of leverage and persuasion you can to get what you want. Good for you, especially if it works. If it does, you may figure that now that you have slain that dragon, you can lean back in your reclining chair and flip through channels for a while. If it doesn't, you may brood for a while in your reclining chair and flip through channels for further evidence that the world is unfair. Either way, you are likely to think that you are done with bringing Me, Inc., to market, at least for a while.

You're not.

Successful people know that the cycle just keeps on cycling. It's not like it used to be, when the pattern was that once you got out of school, you found a job, cut your deal, kept the job, and didn't go back out into the larger marketplace for the rest of your working life.

Today Me, Inc., is pretty much like any other company for sale in public markets. Me, Inc., may encounter the need to cut a deal at any time, or recut a deal that you thought had been put to bed. You've finally gotten to the place where everyone admires your expertise? Sorry, someone else can do it cheaper. You've mastered a skill that took you twenty years to develop? Sorry, a new technology has made it obsolete. You've only worked at this terrific start-up for three months? Sorry, we didn't get our next stage funding. You've been pretty happy where you are, but are starting to think you're getting a little stale? It's time to look for something else. Which means that you need to be in the market all the time because you never know when you are going to be in the third stage of the cycle, cutting yet another deal.

I'll give you a moment to rest after thinking about how demanding that has been and is going to be.

Fortunately, I'm going to tell you how to make it easier instantly and increase your chances of success. And that is by doing what successful people do: working on Steps One and Two all the time, knowing that doing so puts you in much better shape for the third step, or cutting the right deal for you. By keeping up to speed on steps one and two, you will go into step three like a cyclist going down a steep hill with the wind at your back instead of in your face.

Here's how. (Pinks, please be patient with me. This stuff is more abstract, but if you hang in there, I think it will be helpful.)

STEP ONE: CREATE VALUE

Where does value come from? No, I'm not going to talk about the birds and the bees. But like other acts of creation, value usually comes from more than one person. It comes when two people interact. Relationships create value.

Think of the interviews—most of the successful people talked about what they learned from others that enabled them to refine their "offering." Barbara Corcoran talked about how much more effectively she functions because of opposites. Pat Zenner talked about partnering with competitors. Martin Yudkovitz births new entities through joint ventures. Repeatedly, we've seen successful people reaching out for relationships that help them do more and do it better. (Even inventor Alexander Graham Bell had Watson.)

The earlier principles are designed to help you find the people who make you better, who help you find new ways to do things. Learn from your mistakes. See opportunities you might not have otherwise. Balance your weaknesses.

Relationships that are worth investing in make you the best version of you. In other words, if you build and add strong relationships, this version of you would have "New! Improved! More Robust Performance!" written on it in red, white, and blue letters. That's why we spent so much time on the importance of choosing the right people.

Invest in yourself. Once again, let's look at companies larger than Me, Inc., to get our perspective. Imagine two companies in exactly the same business. I don't care what they are. Two ice-cream manufacturers, two e-businesses offering postage stamps, or two diners on the same side of the street. You don't know anything about how these businesses are run except for a single fact: One of the owners takes the profits out of the business and puts them into his or her pocket. The other puts the profits back into the business.

Having only that information, if I said you had to invest money in one or the other of them, which one would you choose? You'd invest in the one that is putting money back into the business, right?

Now let's go back to Me, Inc. If I asked you what you've done lately to invest in yourself, what would you tell me? If you are like a lot of people I hear from, simply hearing the question might make you feel defensive. You would immediately list all the reasons you have for not improving your skills. But investing in your-self can be as simple as spending the time and energy on relationships that work for you.

Let me say that again: Spend your time on relationships that work for you. This may be particularly difficult for you if you are a pink-style person who believes that everyone who asks for a little chunk of you in your work life is entitled to have it. For you pinks, investing in yourself means saying "no" more often. It means that you don't have to say "yes" to every committee, every meeting, or every offer to have drinks after work. It means that you need to say "no" to make enough room to say "yes."

For blue styles, investing in yourself means choosing to pursue relationships. It means lifting your head up from the task for a minute to think about people you want on your team.

Think about Nancy Evans deciding she would get in touch with Candice Carpenter. Or Ken Langone deciding that he wanted to help Bernie Marcus go into business. Or Danny Meyer saying that when he hires people, he looks at the person's people skills first.

If you are navy blue and want to make sure that the relationship-building task has structure and purpose, commit in a serious way to at least one charitable activity. If memory serves, almost every successful person I interviewed was deeply involved in charity and several of them spoke meaningfully about how much they learned from it. Remember Edgar Bronfman's comment about how doing charitable work taught him to listen? Michael Goldstein comes to mind, too. Passionate about charities that serve children, Michael spoke quite movingly about how much more he feels he gets from investing his time in charity than he gives—particularly when he sees children respond to the opportunities money can bring. At the same time, through charitable work, you blues can get to know other people and will be able to see their values in action. That's why it isn't accidental that many successful people end up re-cruiting for their personal board the people they've met through charity and volunteer work.

It may seem odd that the decision to make time for others is one of the most powerful ways to invest in yourself, but successful people know that it is.

STEP TWO: COMMUNICATE YOUR VALUE

Figure out your tag line. Over the years, I've done a lot of consulting work on brand positioning. Putting all the complicated stuff aside, brands are most quickly expressed through tag lines. People have tag lines, too. Think about any popular icon and there's a mental tag: Marilyn, Mel, Madonna, Meat Loaf. It doesn't matter. Lasting stars are the ones that update their tag lines so that they remain compelling.

People have tag lines at work, too. When someone says to you, "Who's Joe?" your answer, and how it's delivered, is Joe's tag line. You have a tag line, too. What's scary is that everyone may know it but you. You should know it.

Moreover, you should understand the value of the Me, Inc. brand so well that you create your own tag line. The good news is that for Me, Inc., as for any other brand, to do that, you only need to figure out two things. The bad news is that figuring these two things out takes a lot of work.

First, you have to figure out what is unique about what you bring to the marketplace. That includes your skills, potential, energy, capacity, and character. Here's a quick exercise to get you started.

Close your eyes for a minute and imagine that you're walking blindly into a business meeting. Someone else set the meeting up, and you don't know much about why you're there, all you know is that you're going to be meeting someone who may turn out to be good for your business and might be joining you as a client (customer, associate, venture capitalist, whatever is appropriate for your current version of Me, Inc.). You go into an unfamiliar office at the prescribed time, you announce yourself to the receptionist, and you are kept waiting for ten minutes.

A very elegant assistant glides out to greet you, guides you down an endless hallway to a private conference room, and the person rising from the table, arm outstretched to shake hands, is Bill Gates (feel free to replace this image with any powerful executive you choose: Lou Gerstner, Oprah, Michael Eisner, Martha Stewart, Warren Buffett; it really doesn't matter as long as it's someone very rich, powerful, and whom you find intimidating).

The big exec sits back in his or her chair, looks you in the eye, and says, "So, I hear you're the one to talk to. I've got twenty-five million dollars worth of business I'm considering doing with Me, Inc. Tell me why I should give it to you. Not your company. You."

Take ten minutes, put your pen to paper, and don't stop writing until you've jotted down at least twenty reasons you should get that twenty-five mil. Don't edit yourself and don't bother phrasing your answers the way you might in a real meeting (i.e., no corporate speak).

Do it now before you read on.

I'm humming the tune from *Jeopardy!* as you write.

It's not easy, is it? Like any other brainstorming exercise, you've probably come up with some great stuff, some mediocre stuff, and a few ideas that are so lame when you read them that you can't believe they ever came into your head.

I gave this assignment to a techie friend who pictured the executive in the room as Bill Gates. His list:

- I'm smart

- I have a lot of good ideas

- I'm trustworthy

- I've never lost $25 million before

- I use Windows 98

- I'm a good listener

- I'm creative

- I've done quite well for people who are a whole lot less important than you

- I follow directions

- But I'm independent

- I will be incredibly appreciative

- I'm fun to be around

- I'll be there at your beck and call

- I've never had trouble with the Justice Department

- I have some great ideas to fix that annoying "Office Assistant"

- I like rain

- I'm energetic

- I have three kids who start college in eleven years

- I'm loyal

- I'm a good communicator

- I've done good work for Apple; if it was successful for an also-ran company like that, imagine what it could do for you

Put the list away for a few days to let it season. Then take it out, look down it closely, and think, item by item, if you really believe that each of the things you listed are things that could be valuable to someone else. Keep editing your list until you get down to a sentence you can say to yourself in the mirror without laughing or wincing. The editing process could take weeks. Hang in there.

You want something you can say in one breath. A reasonable person's breath, not a yogi's. That's your tag line, and it needs to be really succinct. Pretend that you are saying it on air at the Super Bowl and every thirty seconds costs you a million bucks.

Keep your tag line current. Put it up on your bulletin board, or install a shortcut to it on your desktop. When the dark moments come, look at it to remind yourself you do have value—all you need to do is make sure it comes to the attention of the right people.

An Act to Follow

Make Bigger Brand Statements. Tag lines are great, but they're not your most powerful brand communication. In the marketplace, walking away from the wrong opportunities speaks more loudly about your brand than anything you could possibly say.

Successful people often raised this point in my interviews with them. The story that stands out most clearly in my mind comes from Jim Farrell. He was approached for a joint venture on a project that would be worth $50 million to him, but he believed it was ultimately a sham. He turned it down.

Fifty million dollars sounds like a lot of money to me. A *lot* of money. So I asked him why he said no.

"I wouldn't sell my reputation for fifty million dollars. Because reputation is hard to achieve and easy to lose. Very difficult to maintain and extremely easy to get blown up. And once you've lost the reputation, to get it back is a horrendous job."

Remember that, in some ways, your colleagues are like your children. They'll listen to what you say. They'll believe what you do.

Kiss the Right Babies

When I started thinking about this project, I scouted around to see what other people had already said about relationship building in business. There are some great books out there, virtually all of them directed to helping you build relationships with people who fall into a specific category. You can get advice on how to communicate your brand to customers; or what it takes to keep employees with you; how to improve your relationships with vendors; and how to handle joint ventures of all kinds.

These are vitally important skills, but from my perspective, are best addressed after you answer the strategic questions: "Who is it that needs to believe in my value to help me achieve my dream?" and "What categories of people will have the biggest impact on whether or not my vision is realized?"

In marketing and PR, this concept is called understanding your target audience. I like the idea of having a target because it helps you aim your communication arrows, thus avoiding wasting thousands of them by shooting at oranges, plums, and basketballs instead of apples.

If you drag out your old marketing textbooks, you'll remember the fancy way of talking about this, which is to talk about efficiency and effectiveness.

Efficiency means addressing your comments to someone who might have a reason to listen to you; that is, not starting out by trying to sell ice to Eskimos. Effectiveness is just that—telling your story in a compelling way.

For Me, Inc., then, the way to think about efficiency is to think about your constituencies. Pretend you're a politician. Once you know whose vote you need, you know which constituencies are most important and which babies you are going to kiss.

The way you spend your time should also line up with the constituencies that matter most, which harks back to the lesson about the tuna guys. The thing is, tuna guys are a moving target.

Ira Millstein told me a great story about learning how key constituencies changed as he was moving up the ranks of his law firm. An older friend and senior partner in a then major law firm asked him whose calls he was returning and in what order. Ira Millstein, well-trained by now in the importance of client management, thought he knew the answer: "The client's, of course." But it was the wrong answer. The answer was his partners. Why? If he didn't have his partners, he wouldn't have the whole means to represent clients. He needed to motivate his partners, to demonstrate that he cared about them, and to inspire them to care as much as he did about the partnership. As a result of this conversation, he realized that he had to change his priorities, and his partners became his number-one target audience. Remember that every time you make a change, even in the same organization, you will have new constituencies and the relative importance of those constituencies will change over time as they did with Ira Millstein.

When successful people make a change, they also make sure that their new priorities are reflected. Ira Millstein told me that he also had to learn how to demonstrate the new priorities most effectively, i.e., phone calls or dropping by someone's office.

Priorities aren't just defined by how you spend your time. For instance, how you use your space can communicate a message to your target audience. Doors, tables, offices, and chairs tell lots of stories. Recently, I went to a brand-new wellness center in New York. My first impression was that the waiting room was exceptionally nice, with high ceilings, huge windows, lots of light, and big comfy chairs. The administrative offices, including the director's office, were in the back, which had neither windows nor room for comfy furniture. I asked about the arrangement and was told it wasn't casual and that they considered their patients as the most important people and wanted to show that. Can you imagine a more effective way to communicate your priorities? I can't.

Let's look at examples of people who made efficiency decisions and spoke effectively. Barbara Corcoran considers time spent with her team of top sales people a priority. Martin Yudkovitz attends to key members of the other team in joint ventures and in each case, looks at ways to bond with them. Danny Meyer courts his vendors for better, faster service and knows that even simple things like answering the door personally are a way to effectively communicate his gratitude for their work. Colleen Barrett spends time on her customers in ways that can be felt. The first decision on which category of relationships is most important is strategic. Then it is about great execution—the systems and language that are the most effective in getting results.

Think about Me, Inc. Are you talking to the right constituency? Are you using a language or system that reinforces your tag line? Are you losing effectiveness by contradicting yourself—perhaps with space that says you're the most important when your mouth is saying that they are?

BELIEVE YOUR OWN TAG LINE

For many people, one of the biggest barriers to success is the reluctance to communicate about their own value. Talking about your value feels like self-promotion, and, for many of us, anything that smacks of self-promotion feels bad.

For a lot of people, initiating a conversation about why someone else should be interested in Me, Inc., resembles an approach to an ice-cold ocean swim.

Over time, I've run into a lot of people who have an approach to starting these selling marketplace conversations with the same distinct lack of enthusiasm I would have for a December dip.

Here's what I have found. The way to be confident is to take the focus off yourself. I learned this years ago the first time I was on a charity board. (I told you charities were good, didn't I?) At one of my first meetings, we were given a list of names of people who had donated money in the past and were asked to call them and ask for a contribution.

I was terrified. Being a good Midwesterner, it just felt pushy, bad, and wrong. I really, really, really didn't want to do it. Until I realized that it wasn't about me at all. It was about whether or not I believed that the organization I was supporting was doing something worthwhile and was worth the support of others. Every time I picked up the phone, I just mentally kept saying, "It isn't about me."

The fear of telling my story came back again when I started doing television and radio appearances to promote my first book. Talking about my book seemed to be only about me and was pretty scary, until I realized it still wasn't about me. It was about whether or not I believed that what I was saying had value to someone else.

With that in mind, here are some tips to build confidence by moving to a relationship focus:

- Be clear about what you're doing for them. You're doing something good when you let a potential buyer know about something that would benefit them. If you aren't comfortable with the quality of that offering, fix it before you try to tell your story.

- Find out as much as you can about your competition. Search on-line. Talk to your board. Mentally position yourself as an advisor. As in: "You can choose me for this effort, or you could consider X, Y, or Z options. Here is why I offer you more value than you could get else-where."

- Pretend you're somebody else. If someone you love told you he was going to ask for what you're asking for, would you think it was reasonable? If so, your self-doubts are just that. Understandable, but unreasonable. Let them go.

MAKE CREDIBILITY AN ACTION STEP

Credibility comes from minimizing the gap between what you say you'll do and what you actually do. Many of us destroy credibility in thoughtless ways, often because we mean well. We say we are going to call. Or write. Or send something. We mean it when we say it. But somehow we just don't. If our brand is a promise, these are promises that we don't keep.

> "Over time, analysts just figure out, based on the track record of the people who are telling them things, whether eighty percent of what they're being told is likely to come true, or fifty percent will probably come true."
>
> —MICHAEL CULP

Successful people talk a lot about integrity and credibility. I'm not including advice on integrity because you are a grown-up and you either have it or you don't. I can only encourage you by reminding you that integrity does pay off in the long run, while knowing that waiting for it to pay off can take a very long time and can feel like forever.

> "Success? One word. Integrity. End of story. That's it. You may not even succeed at your business but if you did it with integrity and did it to the best of your ability, that's the key."
>
> —CRISTINA CARLINO

Credibility is another thing. You can increase your credibility in two ways.

The first is the signature of successful people: being very careful about what you promise. This is a risk for both pink and blues. One of my former bosses, whom we will call Chip, had a very pink style, which is not unusual in people who are managing sales efforts. You have to be people-oriented to motivate salespeople. Chip had a very strong desire to please. So that no matter what someone asked, Chip wanted to say yes and often did. He always meant it in the moment. It was just that when the next person walked in and Chip announced what he had promised, the response was likely to be: "What, are you crazy?" Chip would be filled with regret and often made matters worse by reversing a decision he'd just made.

Overpromising destroys credibility and makes for bad relationships. When you overpromise, you either don't deliver, which makes the other person unhappy, or you do deliver, but make yourself resentful because you have other reasons you really didn't want to do it. If you recognize yourself in this scenario, go on a promise diet. Don't promise anything for a week. Just say, "Let me think about it."

Esther Dyson has a trick she uses to keep from overpromising that I love so much I copied it. We were talking about how easy it is to say yes to things that seem far out in the future. Before she says yes, Esther looks at a sign hanging in her office. The sign says: "Would you say yes if it were next Tuesday?"

Better to say no now than no at the last minute, which always strains goodwill.

If you are pink, remember that credibility comes from the ability to say no.

If you're blue, credibility strain is more likely to come from overpromising against task ("Sure, I can do two hundred push-ups in less than five minutes!") or from forgetting to tend to relationships at all when under pressure, which will make you look erratic, since sometimes it will feel to others like you are paying attention and other times it won't. Lack of predictability creates lack of credibility.

Another way of looking at credibility is to think of the pleasure that you get when you buy a product that lives up to its marketing. The marketing will get you to buy it once, but the fact that the product delivers what the brand promises will keep you coming back. And it's not just the big deals that you say you're going to close. Things like telling your assistant you'll deal with your overflowing in-box today is good practice and breeds credibility in larger arenas. Remember: Credibility is always a work in progress. Do what you say you're going to do and pretty soon most of Me, Inc.'s, opportunities will come from people who've done business with you before.

Step Three: Let's Make a Deal

Be Worth What You Cost

Okay, so now that you have relationships that bolster Me, Inc., and you know your tag line, we must get down to the nitty-gritty: the conversation between Me, Inc., and possible buyers about what you are worth.

It seems to me that Americans are getting a lot more comfortable negotiating about price. Maybe I have just heard one too many Priceline.com ads, but my sense is that just plain normal folks are getting much more sophisticated about price being determined by what the market will bear.

If we think about a market as a conversation between a buyer and a seller, the Internet has given us all a bigger "room" in which to have those conversations.

As a result, we expect to negotiate about the price of items we used to think of as fixed. Airline tickets, hotel rooms, groceries, designer clothes, and lots of other items we thought of as fixed in price no longer are.

Your price isn't fixed, either, or at least not permanently. If you are an employee, you have some stability in pricing. Your employer pays you X, and unless you do a terrible job and get fired or downgraded, it will stay at X.

But deep in your employer's beady little brain may be the thought, "You know, maybe I could get one just like Me, Inc., at X minus twenty-five percent." Which means that whether or not you are conscious of it, you are being priced against other people like you all the time.

So your price isn't fixed. When you are feeding a family, this is a pretty scary thought. "You mean, I could get less? They could fire me to save the money?" Yes, they could, and they do.

You can fight this reality. You can hate this reality. You can blame bosses, Fat Cats, Republicans or Democrats (or both), economists, or immigration policies. Or you can accept it and make it work for you as much as possible.

The question is: Why can't they just understand that my experience means that I bring value and compensate me for that value at what I consider a fair rate?

Sometimes they can. There's a better shot they will if you help them. To do that, you have to know more about your market value than they do. This is why it's important to develop your tag line, and communicate it and know how it stacks up against others like it in the market.

Understand Relationship Pricing

Soybeans, wheat, and blind-label orange juice are commodity products. Commodity products are those just like any other in their category. With commodity products, the discussion between buyer and seller is only about price. "There's nothing special about this pen or this tape dispenser. I'll give you the least amount for it."

You aren't a commodity and don't want to be priced as one. You are special. You are unique. You add value.

Once you move away from commodity pricing, you start to see the negative and positive effects of relationships in pricing. There sometimes exists in business relationships a seesaw between emotional content and cash. Imagine that you are a free agent, meaning someone who works for themselves. You are on one end of the seesaw. You have just gone into business for yourself and are terrified about whether or not you are going to make it. On the other end of the seesaw is Mongo, your first big client. Mongo suffers from extreme bad attitude. Mongo is critical of everything you do and wants your endless, fascinated attention to every complaint that belches out of Mongo's bellyache of a brain. Mongo only pays after ninety days and doesn't pay very well. On the other hand, Mongo does pay. Mongo's cash is all that is keeping you up in the air. Mongo is worth it.

Time passes. Your cash flow picks up. You attract more clients, including some reasonable ones.

The day comes when Mongo asks you to perform yet another miracle under short notice. You agree.

But agree at a special price. Just as there is relationship pricing, or VIP pricing for reasonable people who treat you well, there is PIB (Pain In the Butt) pricing for Mongo.

Against the advice of this book, some people will continue to be relationship inattentive and may even seem to profit from it. But I can pretty much guarantee that they are paying a higher price than their attentive counterparts for that privilege. A friend of mine is currently looking for a job as an executive assistant. One of the things she has noticed is the PIB premium. One potential PIB boss was so clearly in the category that the offering salary to be his assistant increased week by week as candidate after candidate turned down the job offer. If you're going to be a jerk, be prepared to pay for the opportunity.

Accumulate Relationship Credit

When analysts are evaluating companies, they look at their balance sheets. The best companies manage their balance sheets so that they can weather the inevitable business storms. It is guaranteed that something will come up that slows growth or that chews up a lot of cash: a tornado, a lawsuit, a new competitor, or a giant comet hurtling down from a parallel universe. Which is why there has to be money put aside, but not so much that there isn't any to run current operations and invest in the future.

Your personal balance sheet works much the same way.

Randy Kirk told me a great story about relationships and balance sheets. Randy's father owned several Taco Bell franchises and Randy wanted to buy them. Families being what they are, this wasn't an uncomplicated transaction. Randy wasn't sitting on a pile of money, so just paying cash was out of the question. But it turned out that Randy had something else on his balance sheet of value. The relationship he had with the Taco Bell franchises and the team. He knew them and they knew him. He would be able to walk in there and be productive right away because of the strength of those relationships. With that on his balance sheet, Randy and Taco Bell were able to work out terms that made it possible for Randy to buy his dad out.

Having a personal board and relationships you can count on is important in good times. It is even more important in bad. I've seen it happen over and over again. For example, two senior people I used to work with had similar jobs and lost them within months of each other. One of them was relationship-rich, a man who was known for the efforts he made to help other people out with their careers. Someone who had people he was close to and who made the effort to care. The other one was a traditional user: glib, attractive, full of bonhomie for those above him and disrespect for those beneath him. The first one was back at work at a similar job, but which offered different kinds of opportunities for growth, within six weeks. The other was out of work for fourteen months.

Shorten the Cycle Time

In general, the faster you can bring a product to the market the better. One of the reasons the economy improved during the 1990s was that businesses found a way to get products to the market faster. An ongoing goal for every business is to drive out inefficiencies, or those pesky little problems that keep us from getting tomatoes to the store before they turn to mush, or to get cars on the lot exactly when they are needed, but not before. Speed can be, and often is, a competitive weapon.

So now we are back to Me, Inc., and your job of bringing yourself to the market over and over again. As I've outlined in this chapter, two-thirds of the cycle is getting to the point of negotiation. Before you can negotiate, you have to create something to sell and let somebody know that you have something worth buying. You have to create value and communicate effectively about it.

There are a couple of ways you can do this.

You can start all over again every time the need arises. You can draft a resume from scratch or do a press release or an ad. Then you can try to figure out who might be interested, maybe trying the classic approach of throwing as much informational spaghetti at the wall as possible in hopes that some of it sticks to the right places. To go back to my car metaphor, this approach can and does work, although sometimes it feels like trying to start an old car and get it up to 60 mph within ten seconds on a freezing, early February morning in Chicago.

Or you can apply the nine principles laid out in this book, which is the equivalent of keeping the car warm, in drive, with the motor purring all the time.

TIPS FOR CLOSING RELATIONSHIP-FRIENDLY DEALS

Nothing makes or breaks business relationships like deals. Don't you remember all the times somebody demanded impossible terms from you when they really didn't need to? And the times someone gave you a little extra, just so you would feel good about it?

I'm not going to tell you all about negotiating, but I am going to tell you this: Negotiating the deal is both the final stage in bringing your product to market successfully and the first stage in bringing yourself to market successfully. Because it is never over.

Your goal in negotiating for Me, Inc., is to feel like you've won. Not to feel like they've lost. Every deal that costs the other side too much ends up costing you more, too, eventually.

Here are a few things to remember about relationship-friendly deals. These aren't the deals that flow through every business, all day long, but the ones with people who, for whatever reason, matter to you most.

- **Give them a chance to match the competition's price.** Everyone understands business imperatives. If someone comes to you with a terrific price for the same quality item, no one expects you to honor the relationship at the expense of the bottom line. But they do expect you to give them the chance to compete.

- **Consider pre-nups for complex relationships.** The idea is to talk in advance about how to unwind agreements so that if the moment comes, it isn't the equivalent of a neutron bomb, which leaves the building intact but destroys the people.

- **Give them bragging rights.** Remember, at the end of the day they'd like to go home and brag about it, too. Best of all is giving them something that makes them look good to their boss.

- **Put the incentives where your common interests are.** Whether you are an employer or an employee, a salary just for showing up every day doesn't cut it. Work to find ways to reward behaviors that are good for "us" instead of just "me."

- **Say "next time" instead of no.** No matter how good the relationship, or how much you'd like to build a relationship with someone, sometimes the terms of a deal just aren't going to work for you. In that case, the goal is to get out in a way that teaches the other person what would work for you, so they not only want to come back, but they know what they need to come back with for you to say yes.

- **Expect it to work out.** Marty Yudkovitz finds the following philosophy works best for him: "If you say 'I'm going to make it work out,' you'll have a better chance than if you simply do it on the basis of 'Gee, if this works out, great, and if it doesn't, it doesn't.' "

- **Be willing to leave something on the table.** Winners who take all don't always get asked to play again.

The deal is where the relationship rubber hits the road. It's also where you will be most tempted to trade relationships for cash. If you do, don't sell cheap. Remember that what you're selling is part of yourself.

THE PROMISE OF RICHES

"Everybody's idea of success today is that you make a lot of money. I think success is when you really feel good about what you've done. You feel good about the accomplishment. That's success."

—BERNIE MARCUS

IN THE INTRODUCTION, I PROMISED YOU THAT IF YOU READ THE BOOK and followed the principles, you would be more successful.

Whether you read the book because you want to make more money or because you want your work life to feel more rewarding—or both—the principles will help. But they can only help if you put them to use.

Like dancing, golf, cooking, surgery, or car repair, you won't actually get better at building the right business relationships until you work at it. And like all human skills, the goal isn't to be perfect, it's to keep on getting better.

Now that you've finished the book, you're ready for your to-do list. As a smart business person, you know the only way to get results is to start with a list.

The time has come to put that list together. You are the CEO of Me, Inc., and making a to-do list is your job. You're the only one who knows you well enough to know what needs to be on that list. But, like any good consultant, I do have some advice on getting started.

Realistically, you can only concentrate on one or two changes at a time. Trying to tackle nine things at once is a recipe for disaster. That means that your first decision is to pick one or two of the principles to work on. The easiest way to do this is to pick one that you are really good at, so you can play to your strength by getting even better. Then pick another you suspect that you're not so good at, or that seems to you to be the source of problems.

With those two thoughts in mind, take a look at the following list of principles and proposals. See which ones pop out as you consider your own best and worst and pick a place to start.

For each principle, I've included a couple of recommended tasks, just to give you a sense of how to translate your new understanding into prospects for a more successful career. You'll think of more.

Principle One: Always Remember It Pays to Be Personal

If you've read this far, you've already made the decision to treat relationships as valuable. Give yourself a checkmark on the to-do list. You're done. If your commitment needs occasional bolstering, make yourself a little sign with the following statement and post it where you will see it: "In any business situation where price and performance are equal, the strongest relationship wins."

Principle Two: Obey the Rules of the Role

Two ongoing to-dos here: Monitor your business relationships for signs that you're in trouble and avoid complicating multiple-role relationships to the point that business can't get done. If you work in a family business, with friends, with a romantic partner, or for yourself, this is a principle that's particularly important.

Signs that you may be in role trouble include changes in pattern: Suddenly the other person either withdraws or becomes more aggressive, she seems to want to spend less time with you, or always asks to have a third party involved. When you see signs of role concern, your task is to initiate conversation about role and performance expectations.

Even if things are going swimmingly, check in on multiple-role relationships at least once a month, more often if you are in a fast growth mode. If your organization is growing geometrically, the amount of energy you spend on keeping roles and relationships straight needs to grow at the same rate.

Principle Three: Be Fluent in Both Pink and Blue

The first item on this to-do list is to identify your own style as pink or blue. You've already done it. Another checkmark! Your next task is an everyday thing. Every time you meet someone potentially important, take a moment to figure out if her style is pink or blue and to decide if you need to make a minor style adjustment of your own as a result.

The other to-do comes in to play if you are in a critically important relationship with someone with the opposite style. If you are, your task is to find a way to get regular perspectives on their style from someone else you trust. Like Phil Riese, you may need to hire that ability. Or you can barter for it. My friend Tank, whom I've mentioned before, is someone I turn to for blue-style translations. In return, I'm always happy to help in those rare moments when he is mystified by behavior à la pink.

Principle Four: Choose Your People Like You Choose Your Stocks

This task is ongoing as well, but make a note on your calendar to check progress once a quarter, at least. Your goal is to have about six people in your business life whom you trust and feel comfortable sharing dreams with. The immediate to-do is to stop and list those closest to you in your business life and figure out why they're close. Is it because they're near at hand? Or because they also care about something near to your heart?

Principle Five: Diversify Your Holdings

If you haven't already done so, write down a list of your six closest and most valuable business relationships. Now write down everything you have in common. Do you all work for the same company? Live in the same community? Belong to the same club? Then you know you have work to do to balance your personal board. Now take a look at your tag line (you did develop that after you read Principle Nine, didn't you?). If you were going to compete against that brand, what would you develop? Mentally attack your own brand until you are really clear on its weaknesses.

That tells you the strengths that will be most valuable to you, and the ones that you need to add to your personal board. You don't need to go as far as being able to write personal ads, but you do need to know what kinds of skills and strengths you're looking for in someone else.

The final to-do on this principle is to recruit your opposite to your personal board within the next six months, which is a very aggressive time frame.

Principle Six: Don't Waste Time on the Wrong People

Identify the people in your work life who "cost" too much. Don't go hog-wild here; if there are more than three or four, you've got more serious problems. Figure out how you can spend less time with each one, which includes thinking or talking about them.

Go back to the relationship budget, if need be, and track Category Three time for a week. Your goal is to cut Category Three time down by 25 percent over the next quarter.

Principle Seven: Do It Every Day

Review the systems described and think about which one would be best for you: one that plays to your strengths and doesn't stress your weaknesses. Your contact system should be part of what you naturally do every day. Use Lotus Organizer? Go into the planner and include anniversary dates to prompt yourself to remember special moments. Like to talk on the phone during off hours? Use Ellen Levine's idea of just touching base with someone by leaving a message when you have time over the weekend.

If you can't figure out where to start, begin with the Linda Srere system: Every day, first thing, reach out to someone you are doing business with, someone you want to do business with, or a friend.

That done, commit to "throwing the party" at least once a year. Think about all the ways you could bring together people with common interests. Maybe it's vendors, franchisees, strategic partners, or people who have other reasons to be curious about your industry. Host something, either in person or on-line, that creates value for them. It doesn't have to be a big deal, it can be six people for breakfast. Just take a step toward being the one who makes it possible for other people to meaningfully connect.

Principle Eight: Give Yourself Time to Win

The to-do here is to see if you can handle mistakes more productively. Start with the next three mistakes you encounter. Take a look at how you heard about the mistake. If it was by accident, or after a long time, then it means that someone believes you will punish her for making mistakes. That is never good news.

Tell her that next time you want to be her partner. Admit to one of yours. See if the next time you get better information, sooner.

Next, look at whom you are disagreeing with, and how. Is your style of resolving differences working for longer relationships, or are you just churning through people? Obviously, depending on where you are in your career, relationship tenure will vary. But if your entire "relationship portfolio" is turning over every six to eighteen months, it's a sign that you are having difficulty either raising differences or resolving them. This is a danger sign and means that something needs to change—either you or your environment.

Principle Nine: Do Deals Based on Relationships

If you haven't already written your own tag line, do it now. Remember that the attributes you are looking for are the ones that make life better, easier, and more productive for someone else. Try it out on your board and keep rewriting it as your brand grows.

Now that you have this list, put this book down, pick yourself up, find someone in your business life worth relating to, and go do it.

Make it personal.

ACKNOWLEDGMENTS

My agent, Jan Miller, once told me that I was the luckiest woman in the world. On my good days I believe she is right. But it took more than luck to get on the calendar of highly successful people, and I would like to thank Melissa Berman, Marti Dinerstein, Scott Durkin, Paula Gavin, Bill Higgins, Aven Kerr, Susan Stautberg, Hardie Tankersley, Bill Tremayne, Rochelle Udelle, and Lulu Wang for their help.

My sincere thanks also to everyone I interviewed for this book, including those whose names appear on the Cast of Characters list and those whose names, for various reasons, do not. Special thanks to their assistants as well for their patience and support during the difficult task of scheduling.

Thanks also to Bob Miller, Senior Vice President and Managing Director; Martha Levin, Vice President and Publisher; the book's acquiring editor, Jennifer Barth; and to publicist Jennifer Landers for her insight and enthusiasm. I am also grateful to my Hyperion editor, Peternelle Van Arsdale, for her clarity of insight, steady support, and patience.

Neil Cleary, my gifted editorial assistant, spent more than a year of his life with faxes, phones and e-mails in order to get interviews scheduled, transcribed, and cleared. I suspect that many of the interviews only took place because the person on the other end of the phone justifiably thought so well of Neil. His energy, sensitivity and mellifluous voice constituted the rocket fuel the book needed for liftoff. My research assistant, Lisa Poliak, and word-processing wizard, Mike Johnson, were also tremendous supports. I especially appreciated Lisa's punctilious attention during the book's final edits.

Steven Gershon, webmaster and network czar, and Heidi Krupp, the world's best promotional partner, continue to earn my daily gratitude.

This book also had its own loving family of Hyperion alumnae. Brian DeFiore is not only the father of the two most adorable little girls I've ever seen, but of this book. Brian had the most loving and patient way imaginable of bringing me back to focus, helping me shape the project, and organizing the material. For me, one of the biggest gifts of the book was the chance to work with Brian and to experience what it meant to work with someone of his caliber. I also want to extend an especially warm thank you to Mollie Doyle, who provided hands-on editorial direction and heavy lifting late in the game, when the book needed to be restructured one more time. Having Mollie in my life reminded me that when mixing business and friendship works, it works spectacularly.

My family and friends deserve thanks, as well. Big hugs to Jerry "Tank" Tankersley and his wife, Jane; Carole and Jeffrey Howard, Herb and Barbara Frank, and Rosemary Ellis, who were always there for me. My mom, my brother Myron, and all the other members of my family tribe deserve acknowledgment just because.

William Zangwill, Ph.D., counselor and friend, sparked this book. His perspective on relationship issues and his commitment to absolute honesty forced me to take another look at how I was living my life. That process of exploration fueled my desire to find out more about how to handle relationships better—and thus this book.

Finally, of course, I must thank my husband, Jim. The best way to do this is to recount a very short story. One day a complete stranger walked up to me in a store, looked at Jimmy, asked if we were married, and then said, "Do you have any idea how lucky you are?" The answer is, "I sure do." Thank you, Jimmy, for being my everything.

CAST OF CHARACTERS

By the way, this is the one part of the book that is certain to be out of date by the time it hits print. Movers and shakers move around. The good news is that they are so well known you will be able to find information about them readily.

William F. Aldinger is Chairman and CEO of Household International, Inc., a major provider of consumer financial services in the United States, Canada, and the U.K. Prior to that he was a senior executive with Wells Fargo Bank, San Francisco. In addition to working for Wells Fargo, Mr. Aldinger has also worked for Citibank, New York, and U.S. Trust Company, New York. He is a member of the New York Bar and serves on the boards of directors of MasterCard International, Illinois Tool Works, Inc., and the combined boards of Children's Memorial Medical Center/Children's Memorial Hospital and the Children's Memorial Foundation. He also serves on the Board of Trustees of Northwestern University and the J. L. Kellogg Graduate School of Management.

Robert Annunziata is Chairman of PF.Net Communications, a facilities-based provider of fiber-optic communications infrastructure to communications carriers, Internet service providers, corporations with enterprise network needs, and government entities. He is also Chairman and CEO of Atlantic Telecommunications Enterprise Fund. Recognized throughout the industry as a pioneer of competitive telecommunications, Mr. Annunziata previously served as CEO and Director of Global Crossing. During his thirteen-month tenure, Global Crossing grew to become the world's first global fiber-optic network. He was also formerly President of AT&T's business services group, and spent fifteen years as Chairman and CEO of Teleport Communications Group, which he built from the ground up before selling the company to AT&T for $12 billion in 1998. Mr. Annunziata serves on the board of directors of the YMCA of Greater New York, Log On America, and Coreon.

Colleen Barrett is Executive Vice President—Customer Service of Southwest Airlines, a unique, high-frequency, shorthaul airline well known as an industry leader in customer service. One of Southwest's three Executive Vice Presidents, she supervises an annual budget averaging $202 million. Prior to joining Southwest, she worked for several years as an Executive Assistant at the law firm of Herb Kelleher, Southwest's current Chairman, President, and CEO.

Richard I. Beattie is Chairman of the Executive Committee of Simpson Thacher & Bartlett, where he specializes in mergers and acquisitions, leveraged buyouts, and corporate law and finance. He has participated in some of the larger and more complex financial transactions, including the merger of America Online and Time Warner, the acquisition of Frontier by Global Crossing, and the attempted merger of WorldCom, Inc., with MCI. He has served in the Carter and Clinton administrations, on the New York City Board of Education, and as a trustee of the Carnegie Corporation. He is also a member of the boards of directors of Harley-Davidson and the National Women's Law Center, as well as a member of the Council on Foreign Relations and Vice Chairman of the Boards of Overseers and Managers of Memorial Sloan-Kettering Cancer Center and the Chairman of the Board of Managers of Memorial Hospital for Cancer and Allied Diseases.

Paul Biondi is a Senior Associate at Mercer Management Consulting in Lexington, Massachusetts. He received a Master's in Management at the J. L. Kellogg Graduate School of Management at Northwestern University. He specializes in life sciences and the healthcare industry.

Carole Black, President and CEO of Lifetime Entertainment Services, oversees both Lifetime Television, the leading provider of women's programming, and the Lifetime Movie Network. A veteran television executive and the first woman to head a commercial station in the Los Angeles marketplace, Ms. Black was formerly President and General Manager of NBC 4 in Los Angeles, which, under her direction, rose from second in its market to number one in under two years.

Cathleen Black is President of Hearst Magazines. The first woman to hold this position, she has directed the revitalization of publications such as *Harper's Bazaar, Esquire,* and *Cosmopolitan.* She is also widely known for her leadership of *USA Today* during the 1980s. She helped launch *Ms.* magazine as its first Advertising Manager in 1972 and later as Associate Publisher. In addition to serving on the board of directors of The Hearst Corporation, she is also on the boards of IBM, The Coca-Cola Company, and The New York Botanical Garden. In 1999, *Fortune* magazine ranked Ms. Black number twenty-five on its list of The Most Powerful Women in American Business.

Myrna Blyth is Editor-in-Chief and Publishing Director of *Ladies' Home Journal.* She is currently pioneering *More,* a new magazine for women ages 40–50. Previously a freelance writer and the author of two novels, Ms. Blyth has served as Executive Editor of *Family Circle* and Senior Editor of *Ingenue* and *Datebook.*

Edgar M. Bronfman, Sr., is Chairman of The Seagram Company Ltd., which, in addition to its traditional beverage business, operates a vast entertainment empire through Universal Studios, Inc. (formerly MCA, Inc.). Mr. Bronfman has held the position of Chairman since 1975, and was previously President of Distillers Corporation-Seagrams Limited. In 1994 he resigned as CEO of The Seagram Company and was succeeded by his son, Edgar Bronfman, Jr. Mr. Bronfman is President of the World Jewish Congress and Chairman of The Samuel Bronfman Foundation, Inc.

Michael and Ellen Brooks are President and Owner/Vice President, respectively, of MB Productions, Inc., which provides large-scale video systems to such clients as Madison Square Garden, Carnegie Hall, AT&T, Lucent Technologies, and the WWF.

David Brown is an acclaimed film and television producer, with film production credits including *Jaws*, *The Verdict*, *A Few Good Men*, *Driving Miss Daisy*, and *The Sting*, which won an Academy Award for Best Picture of 1974. He was the recipient of the Irving G. Thalberg Memorial Award in 1991, with his partner Richard D. Zanuck. Currently he is President of The Manhattan Project Ltd., a production company he founded in 1988, which most recently released the film adaptation of Frank McCourt's best-selling memoir, *Angela's Ashes*.

Red Burns is Founder and Chair of New York University's Interactive Telecommunications Program at Tisch School of the Arts and is one of the founders of the New York New Media Association. She is considered to be one of the seminal thinkers in interactive technology and is often called one of the most influential people in new media.

Cristina Carlino is CEO of philosophy, a new cosmetics company based on her personal principles of recognizing individual inner beauty. She is also President of BioMedic, her first venture, which develops skin care procedures and products used by plastic surgeons and dermatologists worldwide. She went on to partner with David J. Watson to form philosophy, which has grown 79 percent each year since its inception. The two companies currently have combined annual revenues of approximately $35 million.

Dick Cavanagh is President and CEO of The Conference Board, Inc., one of the world's leading business policy organizations. Formerly a partner at McKinsey & Company, he has been Executive Dean of the Kennedy School of Government at Harvard University and has served on presidential commissions, transition teams, and corporate boards.

Barbara Corcoran is Chairman of The Corcoran Group, one of the leading residential real-estate agencies in New York City. She was dubbed "the most sought-after broker in New York" by CNN, with a client list that includes Jerry Seinfeld, Robin Williams, Harrison Ford, and Giorgio Armani.

Michael Culp has been in research and research management on Wall Street for twenty-five years. He is formerly a Managing Director, Director of Research, and a member of the Board of Directors and the Operating Committee of PaineWebber, Inc. Previously he held a number of positions at Prudential Securities, including Director of Global Research and Chairman of the Stock Selection Committee. He was also an analyst at E. F. Hutton and Standard & Poor's.

Julie Hembrock Daum is Managing Director of the U.S. Board Services for Spencer Stuart, one of the world's largest international executive search firms, where she has worked with over a hundred boards of directors. She was formerly Executive Director of the Corporate Resource Board of Catalyst, a leading nonprofit organization working to advance women in business, recruiting women candidates for boards of directors. She began her career in 1979 as a consultant with McKinsey & Company in Los Angeles.

Raylene Decatur is President and CEO of the Denver Museum of Nature and Science, one of the largest museums of its kind in the United States, serving two million people annually through a combination of on-site programs and regional outreach. Having worked in the industry since her teens, Ms. Decatur has also held positions of leadership at the Maryland Science Center in Baltimore, and The Academy of Natural Sciences in Philadelphia.

Richard Donner is one of the most successful producers and directors of both films and television in Hollywood, with credits including *The Omen, Superman, Inside Moves, Radio Flyer, Lady-hawke,* and the hugely profitable *Lethal Weapon* series, as well as the television shows *Kojak, Get Smart, The Wild, Wild West,* and *The Twilight Zone.* He is the recipient of the MTV Movie Award for Best Action Sequence for *Lethal Weapon 3.*

Don Duckworth is Chairman and CEO of The CWD Group, a management consulting and investment firm serving a wide array of clients, from Fortune 50 giants to technology start-ups. Prior to assuming his current position, he led two "Global 20" executive search firms, Horton International and Johnson, Smith and Knisely. Considered an expert in the field of intellectual capital, Mr. Duckworth has more than twenty-five years' experience in general management, human resources, and administration with various companies including BP, Standard Oil, and Norton Company. Mr. Duckworth is on the boards of directors of Crystal Insight, Roxco, Impact Hire, e/E Coaching, and Link Staffing Services.

Esther Dyson has been called a "computer guru," "wizard," and "doyenne of the digerati." She is Chairman of EDventure Holdings, Inc., a small but diversified company focused on emerging information technology worldwide, and an active venture capitalist in the U.S. and in Europe. The author of *Release 2.1,* she is widely looked to as an Internet "pattern-recognizer" and was recently named one of The Fifty Most Powerful Women in American Business by *Fortune* magazine. A frequent public speaker, Ms. Dyson sits on the boards of no less than fifteen companies.

Harold Evans has held numerous executive positions in journalism and publishing, most recently Vice Chairman and Editorial Director of the New York *Daily News*, *Atlantic Monthly*, and *U.S. News & World Report*. He is the former President of Random House and the author of the best-seller *The American Century*.

Marty Evans is National Executive Director of the Girl Scouts of the U.S.A., the largest organization for girls in the world. She took the position after a twenty-nine-year career in the United States Navy, attaining the rank of Rear Admiral. During this time she was at the forefront of increasing opportunities for women in the navy, including opening the full range of operational assignments. She has also served as Chief of Staff at the U.S. Naval Academy and was chosen as a White House fellow in 1979.

Nancy Evans is Co-Founder and Editor-in-Chief of iVillage, the groundbreaking on-line community for women, whose IPO valued the company at $1.8 billion. Ms. Evans was the founder of *Family Life* magazine and was previously President of Doubleday Publishing. Prior to that, she was Editor-in-Chief of the Book Of The Month Club and co-host of *First Edition*, the PBS book and author show. She is the coauthor of two books and a contributing editor of *Redbook* magazine.

Jim Farrell is CEO of Illinois Tool Works, a Fortune 500 company, and a $10 billion multinational manufacturer of highly engineered tools, fasteners, and components. He serves on the boards of Allstate Corporation, Sears, and the Quaker Oats Company.

Dr. Harold Freeman, a renowned cancer specialist, is President and CEO of North General Hospital in Harlem. He was Director of Surgery for the Harlem Hospital Center from 1974 to 1999.

Formerly President of the American Cancer Society, Dr. Freeman is currently Chairman of The U.S. President's Cancer Panel and Associate Director of the National Cancer Institute for Health Disparities. He was the 2000 recipient of the Lay Award from the American Cancer Society.

Christina Gold is Vice Chairman and CEO of Excel Communications, Inc., one of the largest providers of telecommunications services in the United States. She is Founder and former President of The Beaconsfield Group, an advisory firm specializing in marketing/distribution strategies. Formerly President of Avon North America, Ms. Gold reached this position after twenty-four years with Avon's Canadian division and is credited with the revitalization of the ailing cosmetics giant. In January of 1997, she was named one of the Top 25 Managers of the Year by *BusinessWeek* magazine. She sits on the boards of directors of ITT Industries, Inc., Torstar Corporation, and Meredith Corporation, and is a Trustee and Vice Chairman of the Conference Board, Inc., and a Director of the Conference Board of Canada.

Michael Goldstein is Chairman of Toys "R" Us, Inc., one of the leading children's retail chains with over $11 billion in annual sales. He has been with Toys "R" Us for seventeen years, serving as CEO from 1994 to 1997. Mr. Goldstein was formerly Senior Executive Vice President-Operations and Finance of Lerner Stores Corporation and, prior to that, he was a Partner of Ernst & Young in New York. He is a Director of Houghton Mifflin, Finlay Enterprises, Inc., and United Retail Group, as well as The National Retail Federation. He is also a Director of the 92nd St. Y and serves as Chairman of the Finance Committee, in addition to his work as a Director of the Special Contribution fund of the NAACP, The Council on Economic Priorities, The Northside Center for Child Development, The State University–Stony Brook Foundation, Queens College Foundation, For All Kids Foundation, and the New York Restoration Project.

Phyllis Grann is President and CEO of Penguin Putnam Inc., one of the world's foremost publishers of English language consumer books. She has served as Vice President of both MCA, Inc. and Simon & Schuster, and has personally edited nearly thirty best-sellers.

Alessandra Gregory works in the office of David Rockefeller. She has also held positions in public relations for classical music organizations in New York City and worked in the Irish parliamentary house.

Robert Gutenstein is Managing Director of Burnham Securities, Inc. He was formerly CEO of Kalb Voorhis & Co., LLC. Mr. Gutenstein is a CFA and member of the Association for Investment Mangagement Research, the New York Society of Security Analysts, the Communications Analyst Group, the Electronic Analyst Group, and the Computer Analyst Group. He is Vice President and a Trustee of Planned Parenthood of Metropolitan New Jersey and serves on the board and is Co-chair of the Daughters of Miriam Home.

Hans Hageman is Executive Director and Co-Founder of The East Harlem School at Exodus House, a private middle school for at-risk children. A graduate of Princeton University and Columbia University's School of Law, Mr. Hageman has served as a New York County Assistant District Attorney and Chief Counsel to the United States Senate Subcommittee on the Constitution. He was the 1998 recipient of the Robin Hood Foundation's Heroes Award.

Jean D. Hamilton is Executive Vice President of The Prudential Insurance Company of America and CEO of the company's institutional business units, which offer group insurance, 401(k), and other retirement services, guaranteed products, real estate, and relocation services, and workplace marketing. Hamilton previously ran the Prudential Bank and Trust Company, the Prudential Capital Group, and Prudential Asset Sales and Syndications, Inc. She joined Prudential in 1988 from The First National Bank of Chicago, where she was Senior Vice President and head of the Northeastern Banking Department. She is also a board member of The Prudential Foundation, Independent College Fund of New Jersey, Women's Economic Round Table, Four Nations, Standing Tall, and Glass Roots.

Suzanne Jaffe is President of S.D.J. Associates, a venture capital and general marketing services consulting business. She was formerly Deputy Comptroller of New York State and served as a trustee of the U.S. Social Security and Medicare Trust Funds. She serves on the board of directors of Axel Johnson Inc., Creative BioMolecules, and Research Corporation, the second largest science foundation in the country.

David Kaiser is currently CEO and Founder of RespondTV. Mr. Kaiser, a twenty-two-year technology veteran, was most recently a senior strategist and Vice President of America Online (AOL). In 1994, sensing the Web's potential, Mr. Kaiser and several colleagues launched Navisoft, an Internet authoring tool company, which was purchased by AOL. At AOL, Mr. Kaiser facilitated mergers, acquisitions, technology licenses, and strategic relationships, most significantly with Netscape, Verisign, IBM, Javasoft, Progressive Networks, and Apple Computer, Inc. In late 1997, Mr. Kaiser's focus shifted to AOL's TV service. Mr. Kaiser was the Founding Vice President of engineering at Kaleida, an Apple/IBM joint venture, and Vice President of engineering at Macromedia. He has also worked at NASA.

Jon Katzenbach, best-selling author of *Teams at the Top, The Wisdom of Teams,* and *Peak Performance,* is an expert on the functioning of teams in organizations. He was formerly a Director of McKinsey & Company, called "the most influential consulting firm in the world" by *BusinessWeek*. He is currently Senior Partner at Katzenbach Partners LLC.

Don Keough is Chairman of Allen & Company, Inc. In the mid-1980s, Keough held top positions at three Fortune 500 companies: President of Coca-Cola, Chairman of Columbia Pictures, and Chairman of Coca-Cola Enterprises. Keough is currently Director of Excalibur and is on the boards of *The Washington Post*, Heinz Co., Home Depot, McDonald's Corp., and USA Networks, Inc.

Marcia Kilgore is Founder and Owner of Bliss Spa, New York City's most fashionable and successful spa. Fast becoming a legendary name, Bliss Spa is hailed across the board both by its celebrity clientele and business world admirers. In 1999, a strategic partnership was announced with LVMH (Moët Hennessy Louis Vuitton). Bliss continues to expand, with new locations in uptown Manhattan and London, a BlissWorld Website, and via their catalog, which reaches over 1 million people.

Randy Kirk is President and Co-Owner of Kirk-Murphy Holding, Inc., Coastal Bagels, Inc., and Coastal Nutrition Corp., with ownership of nearly two dozen Taco Bell franchises, as well as General Nutrition Corp., and Bruegger's Bagel-Bakery franchises.

Parker Ladd is Co-Executive Producer of A&E's *Open Book*, a program featuring interviews with prominent authors. He is director of the LMP Awards and Vice President and Member of the board of directors of Literacy Partners, a New York–based nonprofit organization that promotes adult and family literacy, serving students on both local and national levels.

Ken Langone is President and CEO of Invemed Associates, a Manhattan investment bank he founded in 1974. Mr. Langone was included in *Forbes* magazine's 400 Richest People in America list in March 2000. He serves on the boards of ChoicePoint, General Electric, Home Depot, The New York Stock Exchange, Tricon Global Restaurants, and Unify.

Shelly Lazarus is Chairman of Ogilvy & Mather Worldwide, the advertising agency that handles clients such as American Express, Ford, and Mattel. One of very few women in top-level executive positions in advertising, she oversees an international company with $12 billion in annual billings and has been named one of *Fortune* magazine's Most Powerful Women in Business for the past three years. She recently appeared on the cover of *Fortune* magazine as one of the Top 5 Women in American Business.

Jerry Levin is Chairman of Sunbeam Corporation, whose portfolio of world-class brands includes Coleman, Mr. Coffee, Oster, Powermate, and First Alert. Mr. Levin has also served as Chairman and CEO of The Coleman Company, Inc., and Revlon, as well as Chairman of the Board and CEO of the Burger King Corporation. Mr. Levin is currently on the boards of the Sunbeam Corporation; Revlon, Inc.; Ecolab, Inc; and US Bancorp. His community and philanthropic activities include current and recent board memberships with The New York Philharmonic; Graduate School of Business, University of Chicago; and the King David Society.

Ellen Levine is Editor-in-Chief of *Good Housekeeping*, America's leading women's service magazine, and Hearst Publications's largest title. She made publishing history in 1994 when she became the first woman to be appointed to this position since the magazine was founded in 1885. Previously, as Editor-in-Chief of *Redbook* magazine, she oversaw double-digit increases in both advertising and newsstand sales. She was also formerly Editor-in-Chief of *Woman's Day* and a Senior Editor of *Cosmopolitan*. Ms. Levine has received many professional citations, including the Writers' Hall of Fame Award, the Matrix Award, and election to the YWCA

Academy of Women Achievers. She serves on the boards of the New York Restoration Project, Lifetime Television, the Christopher Reeve Foundation, and the Board of Advisors of New York Women in Communications. She is also Consulting Editor of *O, The Oprah Magazine*.

John Limbert is currently the Deputy Coordinator for Counterterrorism in the U.S. State Department. A career Foreign Service Officer since 1973, he taught political science at the U.S. Naval Academy and was a senior fellow at Harvard University's Center for International Affairs. Before joining the Foreign Service, he taught in Iran, both as a Peace Corps volunteer and as an instructor in English at Shiraz University. Mr. Limbert holds the Department of State's Meritorious Honor Award, Superior Honor Award, and Award for Valor—the last received after fourteen months as a hostage in Iran. He also holds the American Foreign Service Association's Rivkin Award for creative dissent. Mr. Limbert holds a Ph.D. in history and Middle Eastern studies from Harvard University and is the author of *Iran: at War with History* (Westview Press, 1987).

Neil Livingstone is a world-renowned international security expert and Co-Chairman and CEO of GlobalOptions LLC, a crisis management firm based in Washington, D.C. He has managed a wide array of complex problems, from the kidnapping of executives to overseeing sensational divorce cases, carrying out difficult rescues, and creating global intelligence networks. A frequent contributor to television and print news, he is the author of nine books on terrorism, security, and foreign policy.

Bernie Marcus is Chairman and Co-Founder of the wildly successful Home Depot chain of stores, and has been included in *Forbes* magazine's 400 Richest People in America list in 1996–1999. After he and Co-Founder Arthur Blank were fired from the Handy Dan home improvement chain in California in 1978, they formed Home Depot, building it from a single store into a do-it-yourself empire. Currently, each of their 868 stores post average annual sales of $44 million.

Jeffrey S. Maurer is President and COO of U.S. Trust Corporation and its principal subsidiary, United States Trust Company of New York with overall responsibility for more than $85 billion of personal and institutional assets. With a thirty-year career at U.S. Trust, Mr. Maurer oversees all aspects of the business. He is a member of the boards of directors of the Greater New York Insurance Companies, Forbes.com, the advisory board of the Salvation Army of Greater New York, and many other charitable organizations.

Doris P. Meister is Executive Director of the Wealth Management Services Division, Chairman and CEO of Merrill Lynch Trust Company, the fastest growing trust company in America and the nation's largest charitable fiduciary, with over $100 billion in assets. Ms. Meister joined Merrill Lynch from Fleet Financial Group, where she was Executive Vice President and Managing Director of the Private Clients Group. She was also a member of Fleet's Management Committee. She was previously the first Executive Vice President of Christie's auction house, and has twenty-four years of professional experience in the financial world. Ms. Meister is a member of two prominent women's organizations, The Women's Forum and The Committee of 200, as well as a member of the boards of Literacy Partners, ArtsConnection, and Young Audiences.

Cynthia A. Metzler is Founder of The Metzler Group. Ms. Metzler's work focuses on coaching leaders to invent new ways of working and leading to meet the challenges of the ever-changing economy. She works with executives to build and lead higher performing organizations where everyone's potential is tapped. She is also Counsel to Pepper Hamilton LLP providing legal counsel in employment, corporate and college governance, and public policy areas. Ms. Metzler was the Acting Secretary and Deputy Secretary of the United States Department of Labor as well as the Assistant Secretary of Labor for Management and the Associate Administrator of the General Services Administration during the Clinton Administration. She has been the CEO of national and international nonprofit organizations and serves on a number of boards and commissions.

Danny Meyer opened New York's Union Square Cafe in 1985, helping to pioneer an exciting new breed of restaurant pairing excellent food and wine with warm hospitality and outstanding value. Continuing his success, Danny opened Gramercy Tavern in 1994. Both Union Square Cafe and Gramercy Tavern have received numerous accolades—including recognition in the 2000 Zagat Restaurant Survey as New York City's #1 and #2 favorite restaurants, respectively. Capturing the spirit of his first two establishments, Danny opened two more restaurants in the fall of 1998—Eleven Madison Park and Tabla. He has co-authored the best-selling *Union Square Cafe Cookbook*. Among his many honors are the 1996 James Beard Humanitarian of the Year Award and the 2000 IFMA Gold and Silver Plate Awards.

Morton Meyerson is Chairman and CEO of 2M Companies, Inc., a private investment company that he founded. Formerly CEO of Perot Systems, Mr. Meyerson is former President of EDS as well as Co-founder of GuruNet. A pioneer in information services technology, Mr. Meyerson has more than thirty-eight years' experience in the industry.

Ira M. Millstein is a Senior Partner in the international law firm of Weil, Gotshal & Manges LLP, where he practices in the areas of antitrust, government regulation, corporate law, and corporate governance. In addition to his active legal practice, Mr. Millstein is the first Eugene F. Williams, Jr., Visiting Professor in Competitive Enterprise and Strategy at the Yale School of Management. He serves as Chairman of the Joint OECD-World Bank sponsored Private Sector Advisory Group on Corporate Governance and Special Advisor to The World Bank on Corporate Governance. He recently Co-Chaired the Blue Ribbon Committee on Improving the Effectiveness of Corporate Audit Committees. He is an Elected Fellow of the American Academy of Arts and Sciences.

William J. Morin is a recognized world leader in the Human Resources consulting industry, having developed many effective Human Resources management strategies for Fortune 500 corporations for the past twenty-five years. He is currently Chairman and CEO of WJM Associates, Inc., a management consulting business that he founded in 1996, specializing in executive development. For over eighteen years, Mr. Morin was Chairman & CEO of Drake Beam Morin, Inc., the world's leading organizational and individual transition consulting firm.

Thor Muller is an Internet business and software pioneer, having directed and founded a number of start-up companies that have made their mark in the world of new media and e-commerce. He is currently CEO and Co-Founder of Trapezo, an e-commerce service at the center of Internet content-commerce delivery. Previously Mr. Muller was Vice President at frogdesign, Inc., the leading multimedia design firm, following its acquisition of Prophet Communications, a communications firm founded by Mr. Muller.

Tom Neff is Chairman of Spencer Stuart, U.S., one of the world's largest international executive search firms. He is widely regarded as one of the world's most successful corporate headhunters and has placed a number of CEOs, board members, and top-level executives. Prior to joining Spencer Stuart he was a principal in executive search with Booz, Allen & Hamilton. Previously, he was CEO of an information services company and a management consultant with McKinsey & Company in New York and Australia.

Mr. Neff is co-author of *Lessons from the Top: The Search for America's Best Business Leaders*. He serves on the boards of directors of two public companies, Ace Limited and EXULT, Inc., as well as the Lord Abbett mutual funds.

C. William Pollard is Chairman and CEO of ServiceMaster, a consumer and management services corporation that operates through its own brand as well as TruGreen-ChemLawn, Terminix, American Home Shield, and Merry Maids. Since joining the company in 1977, Pollard has led the company from $234 million in customer level revenues to $7.3 billion. He is also Director of a number of educational, religious, and not-for-profit organizations, including Wheaton College, the Drucker Foundation, and the Billy Graham Evangelical Association.

Hugh B. Price is President of National Urban League, Inc., a social service and civil rights organization helping African Americans in achieving economic and social equality through advocacy, research, services, and race relations facilitation. Before taking this position, Mr. Price was Vice President of the Rockefeller Foundation, where he managed domestic initiatives in education for at-risk youth. In the late 1960s, Mr. Price served as the first Executive Director of the Black Coalition in New Haven, Connecticut. In addition, between 1978 and 1982, he was a member of the Editorial Board of *The New York Times,* covering public policy issues including public education, urban affairs, welfare, and criminal justice.

Thomas C. Quick is President and Chief Operating Officer of Quick & Reilly/Fleet Securities, Inc. In 1998, Quick & Reilly became part of Fleet, now FleetBoston Financial Corporation (NYSE: FBF), one of the nation's largest and most successful financial services firms and holding company for one of the nations' largest banks. Mr. Quick is a member of the Board of Directors of FleetBoston Financial Corporation. He serves as a Trustee for the Securities Industry Foundation for Economic Education. He is also a member of the Board of Trustees, the Investment Advisory Board, and the Endowment Committee for the St. Jude Children's Research Hospital, Memphis, Tennessee. He is Trustee and Treasurer of the National Corporate Theater Fund and a Trustee of the Alcoholism Council of New York. He is also a member of the Board of Trustees of Fairfield University and a member of the Board of Directors for Best Buddies. He is a member of the boards of directors of Senesco Technologies, Inc., and Corcoran.com.

Phillip J. Riese is CEO of OptiMark Holdings Inc., a leading provider of exchange solutions to electronic marketplaces and communities. Prior to joining OptiMark in 1998, Mr. Riese was President of the Consumer Card Services Group at American Express, where he and his management team were credited with being largely responsible for the turnaround of American Express's core business in the U.S.

Lauren Shuler Donner is a hit-making Hollywood producer with film credits including *You've Got Mail*, *Any Given Sunday*, *Dave*, *Free Willy*, *Mr. Mom*, *Pretty in Pink*, and *St. Elmo's Fire*. Her most recent film release was *X-Men*. She has been twice honored by her alma mater, Boston University, with a Distinguished Alumni Award in 1987 and again in 1993 in the category of "Service to the Profession." She currently serves on BU's Executive Committee. Ms. Shuler Donner is on the Board of Directors of the environmental organization TreePeople. She also served as a member of the Executive Committee of the Producer's Branch of the Academy of Motion Pictures Arts and Sciences for eight years (the term limit) and is on the Advisory Board of Women in Film.

Stephen B. Siegel is Chairman and CEO of Insignia/ESG, Inc., the nation's third-largest commercial real-estate services company, and President of the parent company, Insignia Financial Group, Inc. He has orchestrated a major national growth strategy for Insignia/ESG—long the preeminent commercial brokerage in the New York metropolitan area—already among the nation's largest at more than 230 million square feet. Previously, he spent twenty-seven years at Cushman & Wakefield, Inc., achieving the title of Chairman and CEO. Mr. Siegel is highly active in industry and professional associations and is a member of the boards of directors of two Real Estate Investment Trusts: Liberty Property Trust and Tower Realty.

Hardwick Simmons is President and CEO of Prudential Securities, Inc. He began his career in the securities industry in 1966 with Hayden Stone, a predecessor firm of Shearson Lehman Brothers, Inc., holding a number of positions as the firm evolved. Prior to joining Prudential Securities in 1991, Mr. Simmons was President of the Private Client Group at Shearson Lehman Brothers, Inc. He is a member and former Chairman of the Securities Industry Association and a Director of the New York City Partnership and Chamber of Commerce, Inc. He is a trustee of the South Street Seaport Museum, President of the Board of Trustees of the Groton School, and a trustee of the Rippowam Cisqua School in Mt. Kisco, New York.

Liz Smith is a renowned syndicated columnist for *Newsday*, the *New York Post*, and the L.A. Times Syndicate. Her career in journalism spans over fifty years. She has worked for *Cosmopolitan* and *Sports Illustrated* and has also been an associate producer and commentator for CBS Radio, NBC-TV, FOX-TV, and E! Entertainment.

Don Soderquist is Senior Vice Chairman and COO of Wal-Mart Stores, Inc., the mega chain with $165 billion in sales in fiscal 2000. He joined Wal-Mart in 1980 as Executive Vice President. Prior to that he served sixteen years with Ben Franklin, including six years as President and CEO. In 1990 Mr. Soderquist received the Outstanding Business Leader Award from the Northwood Institute in Palm Beach, Florida, and in 1996 he was inducted into the Retailing Hall of Fame. He serves on the Board of Directors of Wal-Mart Stores, Inc., and First National Bank and is Past Chairman of the International Mass Retail Association, as well as Chairman of the Board of Trustees of John Brown University and Past Chairman of the Board of Governors of Children's Miracle Network.

Linda Srere is President of Y & R Advertising, one of the world's preeminent advertising networks. Srere was named one of the 50 Most Powerful Women in American Business by *Fortune* magazine, and one of New York's 100 Most Influential Women in Business by *Crain's New York Business*. Ms. Srere is a member of the board of directors of TheStreet.com.

Leigh Steinberg is a legendary sports agent upon whom the Academy Award–nominated film *Jerry Maguire* was based. He has personally negotiated over $2 billion in deals, including the highest-paid player in the NFL. His firm, Steinberg, Moorad and Dunn, based in Newport Beach, California, represents some of the top athletes in football, baseball, and basketball, and specializes in maximizing their clients' compensation while assisting in their growth into well-rounded role models. The firm has recently added an entertainment management division. Mr. Steinberg is the author of *Winning with Integrity*.

Donald M. Stewart is President and CEO of the Chicago Community Trust. He has been President and CEO of The College Board, which aids students in the transition from high school to college and sponsors the SAT and Advanced Placement Program, for over twelve years. On sabbatical for a year, he served as Senior Program Officer and Special Advisor to the President of The Carnegie Corporation, a general-purpose, grant-making foundation established by Andrew Carnegie, which awards $60 million in grants each year. Mr. Stewart was formerly President of Spelman College in Atlanta, Associate Dean of the Faculty of Arts and Sciences at the University of Pennsylvania, and held a number of international positions with the Ford Foundation.

Alair Townsend is Publisher of *Crain's New York Business*, an award-winning weekly newspaper reporting on the New York City area economy and business community. She became Publisher in 1989, following a career in federal government in Washington, D.C., and in New York City government. She is Vice Chairman of the New York City Partnership and Chamber of Commerce, a board member of Lincoln Center Inc. and Armor Holdings Inc., and is on the Business Council of New York State.

Alberto Vitale is former Chairman and CEO of Random House, Inc., the world's largest English-language trade book publisher. Mr. Vitale has spent twenty-five years in publishing with executive positions at Bantam, Doubleday and Dell and then at Random House. He currently serves as Chairman of the International eBook Foundation, an organization that will select and award the Frankfurt eBook Awards, designed to honor literary achievements in e-publishing in the emerging eBook industry.

Martin Yudkovitz is President of NBC Digital Media and an Executive Vice President of NBC. He is responsible for devising NBC's new media strategy, developing new growth business and ventures, and supervising NBC's established Internet interests, which include NBCi, MSNBC, CNBC.com, the NBC Internet Strategic Investment Portfolio, and the Enhanced Broadcasting Group. He has held several strategic development, business affair, and legal positions within the company since joining NBC in January 1984.

Patrick Zenner is President and CEO of Hoffmann-La Roche Inc., a leading research-intensive pharmaceutical company. He has spent his entire career there, having joined the company as a sales representative in 1969. In 1988, Mr. Zenner was elected to the U.S. company's Executive Committee and Board of Directors and appointed Senior Vice President of the company's pharmaceutical division. In 1993, he was named President and CEO. He recently completed his tenure as the first Chairman of the HealthCare Institute of New Jersey and currently serves on the boards of directors of the Pharmaceutical Research & Manufacturers of America (PhRMA) and the Biotechnology Industry Organization (BIO). He is a member of the American Foundation for Pharmaceutical Education, the Health Care Leadership Council and the National Committee for Quality Health Care.